Download the New In Chess app:

- get early access to every issue
- follow every move on the built-in board

Read New In Chess on your tablet, smartphone or Windows PC, two weeks before the printed edition is available, and replay all the moves in the interactive chess viewer

You can now download the digital edition of New In Chess on your tablet, phone or PC/notebook and read all the stories immediately after publication. By simply tapping on the games you can replay the moves on the interactive chessviewer. So from now on you don't need a board and set to fully enjoy what top grandmasters have to say about their games! The New In Chess app installs in seconds, has all the right features and is easy to operate. We have made an entire issue available as a FREE DOWNLOAD.

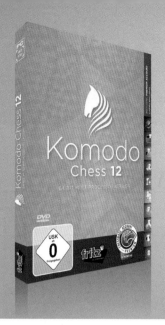

KOMODO 12

Komodo gets going! The new version of the multiple world champion program not only plays stronger than ever. What's more, the additionally supplied „Monte Carlo" version of Komodo 12 uses the analysis technology employed by the AI project „AlphaZero" in its recent sensational match triumph.

In computer chess there is no getting past Komodo: Komodo is a triple TCEC Champion. Last year Komodo won the computer rapid chess world championship with an incredible score of 96%! But what does the surprising success of the AI project AlphaZero mean for the future of computer chess? Will the classical engines, with in addition to cunning algorithms any amount of human chess knowledge, still manage to keep their nose in front? Or will the "Monte Carlo" process win through, which works with huge numbers of games and statistical evaluations?

The new Komodo 12 may have no answer to this question but it does have two engines up its sleeve! For with Komodo 12 you get on one hand the new and improved classical Komodo engine. The developing team of computer expert Mark Lefler and chess grandmaster Larry Kaufman has cranked up the playing strength of the top program a bit further. And on the other hand a Komodo 12 "Monte Carlo" version is included. Here the engine behaves quite differently in analysis: within a short time it plays a whole series of games against itself and comes to its evaluations based on the results of these games. As for playing strength, the "Monte-Carlo" version is not yet up there with the classical Komodo 12. But what is interesting is that the playing style of the two versions clearly differs: the "Monte-Carlo" version plays clearly more aggressively and thus also bases its play less on

„I am deeply moved by the style of Komodo. In my opinion it's the perfect combination between computer accuracy and human positional understanding. I get the feeling it's taken positional understanding to the next level. After such an impressive performance I am going to test Komodo in my future work, especially in very positional play, and am really looking forward to working with it."

GM Boris Avrukh

the material balance on the board. Komodo 12 is thus two things: an absolutely top program and an exciting analysis partner, which will often surprise you with its suggestions and introduce you to interesting ideas!

It is delivered with the new program interface of Fritz 16 and premium membership (6 months) for the ChessBase Account, including access to playchess.com, ChessBase Video-Portal, LiveDatabase, and much more.

KOMODO CHESS 12:
- Improved Komodo 12 multi-processor engine
- New Komodo 12 "Monte Carlo" engine
- New Fritz 16 program interface
- 6 months ChessBase Premium Account

89.90 €

System requirements:
Minimum: Dual Core, 2 GB RAM, Windows 7 or 8.1, DirectX11, graphics card with 256 MB RAM, DVD-ROM drive, Windows Media Player 9 and internet access.
Recommended: PC Intel i5 (Quadcore), 8 GB RAM, Windows 10, DirectX11, graphics card with 512 MB RAM or more, 100% DirectX10-compatible sound card, Windows Media Player 11, DVD-ROM drive and internet access.

ChessBase GmbH · News: en.chessbase.com · CB Shop: shop.chessbase.com
CHESSBASE DEALER: NEW IN CHESS · P.O. Box 1093 · NL-1810 KB Alkmaar
phone (+31)72 5127137 · fax (+31)72 5158234 · WWW.NEWINCHESS.COM

2018#5

NEW IN CHESS

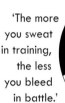

'The more you sweat in training, the less you bleed in battle.'

CONTRIBUTORS TO THIS ISSUE
Simen Agdestein, Bassem Amin, Pal Benko, Jeroen Bosch, Maxim Dlugy, Anish Giri, John Henderson, Dylan McClain, Peter Heine Nielsen, Maxim Notkin, Arthur van de Oudeweetering, Judit Polgar, Hans Ree, Matthew Sadler, Sam Shankland, Nigel Short, Wesley So, Jan Timman, Ju Wenjun, Jilin Zhang

The Road to Kathmandu

t's often said that stepping off a plane into Kathmandu is a pupil-dilating experience, a riot of sights, sounds and smells that can quickly lead to sensory overload. There are a thousand of Kathmandus, all layered together in an extravagant morass of chaos and sophistication, as Alina l'Ami, the intrepid chess photographer and traveler, discovered.

She caught all of this through her lens during a chess simultaneous held in the beating heart of the old city, known as Durbar Square, that was part of a series of World Heritage Program funderaises

awareness initiatives (with various activities, such as cycling, photography and chess) to help rebuild the city following the devastation of the 2015 earthquake.

The simul coincided with the end of the 1st Kathmandu International Open, and this allowed more players to take part and to 'soak up' this historic part of the city. Yet despite being caught out by a torrential and unexpected downpour of rain, that initially saw the event being cancelled, the legendary Nepalese spirit prevailed, and a free simul of sorts, by Ukrainian Grandmaster Konstantin Tarlev, did take place. ∎

Whole Lotta Mate

As the lead singer of Led Zeppelin, Robert Plant carried some of rock's most celebrated anthems. It's hard to imagine Zeppelin classics such as 'Whole Lotta Love', 'Immigrant Song' or 'Rock And Roll' without the power, agility and subtleties of Plant's vocal prowess. But at

Robert Plant: Since I've been loving chess...

69, the living rock 'n' roll legend has reinvented himself, morphing from a tight-trousered rock dinosaur to a more thoughtful artist happy to embrace world music, country and... chess!

In the June edition of *Mojo*, the music magazine's regular 'On The Road' feature was on the Zeppelin former frontman, as he embarked on a US East Coast tour with his current band, The Sensational Space Shifters. With award-winning photographer Pieter M. van Hattem in tow, rock journalist Andrew Perry met up with Plant at his hotel in New York City, only to discover there was no superstar-status kerfuffle, only mild concern that he would be late for – of all things – a midday chess lesson he was looking forward to at the Chess Forum, an Arab-run shop-front in the heart of Greenwich Village, in downtown Manhattan. 'Sipping on a latte,' writes Perry, 'he explains how he chanced upon this place after arriving Stateside a few days early to acclimatize for the current tour, and

duly signed up for a refresher course here, with a Maghrebi tutor, from Casablanca.'

But why chess, asks Perry? 'Because it's good for the brain, innit?' Plant reasons simply. 'The teacher guy kept saying to me, "Why did you do that move – are you a fool?" I said, (*shrugging*) Yes, I probably am.'

A beautiful game

On the eve of the World Cup in Russia, a series of photographs remembering the life of footballer Bobby Moore both on and off the pitch went on display during a new exhibition at London's National Portrait Gallery. Running through January 2019, *Bobby Moore: First Gentleman of English Football*, features family photographs tracing his career, many of which had never been seen in public before.

The West Ham and Fulham legend, who died in 1993 aged 51, captained England to victory over West Germany at Wembley in 1966. While the image of Moore lifting the old Jules Rimet trophy is iconic, the prints provide an insight into lesser-known sides of his personal and professional life.

One print that piqued our interest was taken during the mid-1970s

Franz Beckenbauer and Bobby Moore: who is defending and why?

by the fabled 'Swinging Sixties' snapper, Terry O'Neill. It's a photo of Moore and his German counter-

part Franz Beckenbauer, two of the best defenders in the history of the beautiful game, engrossed in a game of chess in the garden of Moore's Essex home.

Being Pragg-matic

He came close, but not close enough. Several times we wrote about Rameshbabu Praggnanandhaa, the little Chennai wunderkind better

Different generations in the Champ's study. While 'Praggu' admires the chess set, Vishy Anand is looking for the latest verdict on the starting position.

known to everyone as 'Praggu', and his odyssey to break Sergey Karjakin's youngest-ever grandmaster record of 12 years and seven months exactly, set in 2002. Alas, to no avail, but certainly not without a valiant effort on Praggu's part.

At times you just have to be, well, pragmatic when you miss out on a goal – and although Praggu didn't quite manage to break Karjakin's remarkable record, at the 4th Gredine Open, in the small Italian town of Ortisei, he finished on a score of 7½/9 to not only share first place but also, at the age of 12 years, 10 months and 13 days, to become only the second player in history to achieve the GM title before the age of 13 years.

In fact, when Praggu walked into the playing hall for his penultimate round game against Italy's Luca Moroni Jr., he had no clue that there was a possibility of a third and final norm. 'I didn't tell him,' his coach RB Ramesh said during an interview with ESPN India. 'I never talk about norms to players during tournaments because it just puts them under needless pressure.'

Praggu's efforts didn't go unnoticed either back home in Chennai, where his chess hero, Vishy Anand, heaped praise on the country's latest Grandmaster, saying it was a 'fantastic achievement' to earn the title at such a young age. Not only that, but Anand also invited Praggu to come visit him at his home on his return from Italy.

'There are some people who you start liking immediately and Praggu is one', said Anand, who was 18 when he became India's first Grandmaster. 'It may be because he is young.'

Hoop Dreams

For those hoop fans who watched the Golden State Warriors sweep the Cleveland Cavaliers 4-0 to claim the 2018 NBA Finals recently, you may well have revelled in the fact that their talismanic guard Klay Thompson is not only a top defender but also one of the greatest shooters in the history of basketball. You might also be equally impressed to discover that he's also a big chess aficionado and Magnus Carlsen fan!

In late May, Thompson was profiled by Ben Cohen for the *Wall Street Journal*. He explained that the roots of his love for the game can be traced back to a class he took in seventh grade at Riverdale Grade School in Portland, taught by five-time Oregon state champion Carl Haessler. He took the class, he recalled, just to waste time, but quickly realized he was having a great time. Thompson now plays chess as often as he plays basketball: almost every day. 'It's a great game,' he told Cohen. He owns multiple chess boards at home. He carries a magnetic chess set on road trips. And he juggles several chess games on his phone.

And it seems that the chess bug has also caught on with several of his team mates – and so much so that they decided to enlist the services of none other than World Champion and NBA super-fan Magnus Carlsen to pass on some chess tips to them. Cohen reports that Carlsen was in Houston in early May for the Western Conference Finals to take

Sometimes Klay Thompson feels he is living in a dream world...

in a game between the Warriors and the Rockets. Thompson introduced himself to Carlsen as the best chess player on the Warriors, according to his own official locker room rankings.

'Based on loose facts,' he said, 'but whatever.'

Tee time

We all know that chess is a big hit in the world of hip hop thanks to the efforts of RZA, the de facto leader of the chess-mad Wu-Tang Clan. But now on the scene comes the new Detroit rap sensation, Tee Grizzley, who is also endorsing chess as a big educational tool in the inner-cities.

According to *The Fader*, a NYC-based music magazine, the larger-than-life character plays chess the way some people play one-on-one basketball: accompanied by a stream of jovial trash-talk. But he's on a mission to helping high schoolers from tough backgrounds looking to pursue higher education with some-

thing special and different – a lesson in chess and life from an artist who knows his fair share about both.

To that end, he was enlisted as a chess instructor by the Shawn Carter Foundation, run by Gloria Carter, mother of Jay-Z (an avowed Grizzley fan), with a new chess course for dozens of students from New York City looking to possibly attain a college degree. 'In chess, you gotta come up with a strategy,' begins Grizzley, after Ms. Carter has shushed the crowd. 'I made a lot of plans in my life. I'ma do this, I'ma do that, this is gonna happen, that's gonna happen. And a lot of stuff don't go as planned. You really gotta act on events as they unfold. That's how I compare chess to life.'

Grizzley grew up on Joy Road on Detroit's West side and its notorious criminal elements. After a second arrest, he landed in prison. It was there that the rapper first encountered chess, learning from an older inmate 'so cold-blooded he wouldn't give you a single pawn for nothing.' But it was through playing chess in prison that Grizzley not only got good at the game but also began to think through the long-term consequences of his criminal actions. And on his early release, after doing a deal

Tee Grizzley discovered that chess pieces move in miraculous ways.

with the prosecutor, he changed his way. Prison allowed him to write his debut mixtape *My Moment*; and he filmed the video for his breakout single 'First Day Out' on his actual first day out. ∎

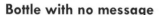

Bottle with no message

Allow me to make a comment about the report on the Berlin Candidates in New In Chess 2018/3, where it is suggested that at one of the press conferences I showed a bottle half filled with urine. I am sorry to disappoint, but the bottle I showed simply contained home-made tea.

The association with urine didn't even cross my mind until I read a comment under the Grischuk Thug Life video on YouTube. Actually, it remains unbelievable for me that anyone could think this way. Therefore I would like to correct this impression, as I wouldn't like your readers, or anyone else, to think I am mad in such a way.

Alexander Grischuk
Moscow, Russia

Reuben Fine (1)

I can add a footnote to 'The double genius of Reuben Fine', New In Chess 2018/4.

Shortly after the Fischer-Spassky match, the book publisher David McKay Company asked me to evaluate a manuscript submitted by Fine. It consisted solely of his annotations of the world championship match.

The notes were dreadful. Fine repeatedly overlooked simple tactics and misunderstood modern openings. I pointed this out to McKay and said that the corrected manuscript could attract readers if it included Fine's view of the psychological aspects of the match.

Big mistake. What Fine added was a bizarre collection of insights. Among those in the published book, *Bobby Fischer's Conquest of the World's Chess Championship*, – Fischer almost always plays for a draw and chooses openings which guarantee 'at least easy equality'. Virtually all of the innovations in the match came from Spassky. Fischer 'hardly prepared at all' because he was 'enormously apprehensive' about the match. Spassky was 'obsessed with an excessive desire' to retreat his pieces (Fine cited 7.♘f3-d2 in a Modern Benoni of Game 3). This corresponds with Spassky's wish to lose the match. Both players had a strange compulsion to move pieces to the edge of the board and advance rook pawns. Spassky revealed his 'curious ambiv-

---

Write to us
New In Chess, P.O. Box 1093
1810 KB Alkmaar, The Netherlands
or e-mail: editors@newinchess.com
Letters may be edited or abridged

---

alence about chess' by having been educated by trainers. 'Chess players do not ordinarily look for trainers', Fine wrote. 'In fact, I have never heard of one apart from Spassky.' And, Fine concluded, 'Certainly Fischer will never retire from chess.'

He added a distorted history of the world championship and recycled his views on the psychology of chessplayers. The result was perhaps the worst chess book ever written by a world class player.

Andy Soltis
New York, NY, USA

Reuben Fine (2)

The article 'The double genius of Reuben Fine' by Joseph G. Ponterotto and Irina Krush in New In Chess 2018/4 provided much food for thought. I am intending to incorporate a considerable amount of the information into revisions I am making to the text of his biography (published 2004, a paperback edition is due this year but will not contain any corrections or additions: there are quite a few of both).

Fine's score in tournament games against Reshevsky was +1 -4 =14. At the National Rapid Transit Championships 1942-4, played at 10 seconds per move, Fine made a perfect 3/3 in games with his *angstgegner*. They drew one 1950 blindfold exhibition game, Reshevsky won an exhibition game in 1951 and their Hall of Fame game in 1986 was also drawn, after a long attempt from Fine to wrest the full point. The second game between the players (Round 1, Pasadena, 1932) Fine later claimed he had adjourned in a won position but was awarded a loss after failing to show up for a resumption rescheduled to accommodate a Jewish Holiday, which Reshevsky intended to observe. In his biographical collection of Reshevsky's games, Stephen Gordon, however, simply states that Reshevsky '... beat an out-of-sorts Fine'. In the absence of the gamescore, a contemporary account of the circumstances would be invaluable.

According to my research, there was no Jewish Holiday between 15 and 28 August 1932, but it could simply be that Fine is referring to Shabbat. It is interesting to note that Reshevsky's losses to Alekhine and Kashdan were both on Saturdays, 20 August and 27 August respectively. His opponents were, of course, two of the strongest players in the world at that time.

Since only a single point separated Dake, Reshevsky and Steiner (3rd-5th) from Bernstein, Factor, Fine and Reinfeld (7th-10th) in the final tournament crosstable at Pasadena, a different result in the game between Fine and Reshevsky would have considerably altered the outcome, for these two players at least.

Almost all of the games between Fine and Reshevsky were hard-fought, with the exception of their last competitive encounter at the Wertheim Memorial, New York, 1951.

As to Fine's memory, I believe that most likely someone with a deep knowledge of a subject is able to rapidly and efficiently assimilate and process new information but that 'photographic memory' has not been scientifically demonstrated. After reading the article, I contacted Dr. Ponterotto about this matter and he replied '... you are likely correct in that research has not really supported

---

the concept to my knowledge, as they have eidetic memory in a small percentage of children. I used the term as it was mentioned by one of his colleagues and former students at his psychoanalytic institute.'

The games annotated by Grandmaster Krush were played not in Hilversum but elsewhere: possibly the error was introduced by that blessing and curse – the database. The first round of the A.V.R.O. tournament was held in Amsterdam and the second in Den Haag (The Hague).

Aidan Woodger
Halifax, West Yorkshire, England

Shamkir and Walter

The article on the Vugar Gashimov Memorial in Shamkir in New In Chess 2018/4, I read with pleasure and interest. Erwin l'Ami did a great job, because his annotations of the game Carlsen-Topalov are both lucid and accurate (having struggled with the same task, I can appreciate it!). I nevertheless discovered one inaccuracy. Black's position was tenable even after the time-control. Without going into great depth, I would like to stress that Black needed to transfer the rook to h6 or f6 to create a fortress. The final mistake was **42...♔g8**, as in that position

Carlsen-Topalov
Shamkir 2018
position after 42.♕c7

Black could still have saved the game, playing 42...♖f1!! 43.♔xg4 (43.♕e7 ♖xf5!? 44.♕xe8 ♖f3+ 45.♔xg4 ♖xc3 is a tablebase draw) 43...♖g1+ 44.♔f4 (or 44.♔f3) 44...♖h1!!

ANALYSIS DIAGRAM

followed by ...♖h6, ...♗c6. It is important that White cannot push f5-f6 because of the check on f1. This resource is extremely difficult for both humans and computers to find, but it is nevertheless fairly relevant. I published this line in the German magazine *Schach*.

Furthermore, I generally quite like the annotations of Anish Giri, but I was not very happy about the following lines at the end of the game Giri-Navara from the same Shamkir tournament: 'I read that after the game my (very pleasant and kind!) opponent blamed this loss and his unfortunate blunder on the fact that he had spent four hours preparing for this game and was not fresh.'

I mentioned that tiring preparation during the press conference (in Anish's presence), when replying to the question about the nature of my blunder (or of my recent losses). At the same time I admitted my own responsibility for it. Anyway, I apologized to Anish on the next day, as he apologized to me after he learnt about my objections to his text.

Finally, I would like to note (see page 15 of the same issue) that the real first name of 'Walter' Buffett is Warren.

David Navara
Prague, Czech Republic

Freedom of the press

How many magazine editors allow their writers such freedom to express themselves as those of New In Chess? For example, I could cite

your toleration of Nigel Short's unrelenting rudeness and pretentious writing style in his wittering about Twittering.

However, it is the refreshingly honest article by Hans Ree in New In Chess 2018/3 which gladdened my heart. Instead of the intended book review he records some painful memories of his chess career, presented alongside an eclectic group of interesting stories. Delightful stuff!

It was very brave of him to reveal the trauma he experienced after the loss of a game in 2001. We are all brought to our knees from time to time by seemingly trivial events. We might be able to cope with our traumas if only we could explain the process of cause and effect clearly. But, embarrassingly, we can't and that makes us feel inadequate to boot.

So let's stop overthinking and let New In Chess distract, enlighten and send us on a voyage of discovery instead. Life is too Short!

Richard Sugden
by email

COLOPHON

PUBLISHER: Allard Hoogland
EDITOR-IN-CHIEF:
Dirk Jan ten Geuzendam
HONORARY EDITOR: Jan Timman
CONTRIBUTING EDITOR: Anish Giri
EDITORS: Peter Boel, René Olthof
PRODUCTION: Joop de Groot
TRANSLATORS: Ken Neat, Piet Verhagen
SALES AND ADVERTISING: Remmelt Otten

PHOTOS AND ILLUSTRATIONS IN THIS ISSUE:
Alina l'Ami, Lennart Ootes, Collection David DeLucia,
Frank Revi, Ye Rongguang, Berend Vonk

COVER PHOTO: Chinese Chess Federation

© No part of this magazine may be reproduced, stored in a retrieval system or transmitted in any form or by any means, recording or otherwise, without the prior permission of the publisher.

**NEW IN CHESS
P.O. BOX 1093
1810 KB ALKMAAR
THE NETHERLANDS**

PHONE: 00-31-(0)72-51 27 137
SUBSCRIPTIONS: nic@newinchess.com
EDITORS: editors@newinchess.com
ADVERTISING: otten@newinchess.com

WWW.NEWINCHESS.COM

Women's Title Matches Are Rarely Dull ...

Unlike in matches for the overall World Championship, the matches for the Women's World title often have a high percentage of decisive results. For example, in the recent match between Ju Wenjun and Tan Zhongyi, half the games were decisive, whereas in the 2016 match between Magnus Carlsen and Sergey Karjakin, 25 percent of the games (including Carlsen's two victories in the playoff) ended decisively.

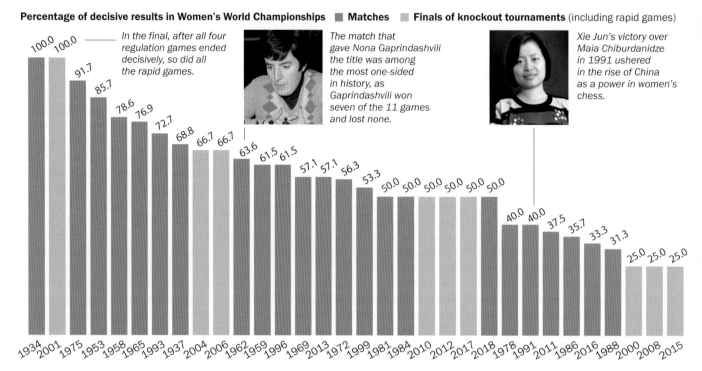

Percentage of decisive results in Women's World Championships ■ **Matches** ■ **Finals of knockout tournaments** (including rapid games)

In the final, after all four regulation games ended decisively, so did all the rapid games.

The match that gave Nona Gaprindashvili the title was among the most one-sided in history, as Gaprindashvili won seven of the 11 games and lost none.

Xie Jun's victory over Maia Chiburdanidze in 1991 ushered in the rise of China as a power in women's chess.

Year	Value
1934	100.0
2001	100.0
1975	91.7
1953	85.7
1958	78.6
1965	76.9
1993	72.7
1937	68.8
2004	66.7
2006	66.7
1962	63.6
1959	61.5
1996	61.5
1969	57.1
2013	57.1
1972	56.3
1999	53.3
1981	50.0
1984	50.0
2010	50.0
2012	50.0
2017	50.0
2018	50.0
1978	40.0
1991	40.0
2011	37.5
1986	35.7
2016	33.3
1988	31.3
2000	25.0
2008	25.0
2015	25.0

... and the Title Is Increasingly Dominated by China

The Soviet Union had a lock on the Women's World Championship, although some of the women playing under its flag were not ethnically Russian (the notable examples being Nona Gaprindashvili and Maia Chiburdanidze, both of Georgia). The rise of Xie Jun of China changed that and, in recent years, she has been followed by a string of talented Chinese players, the best being Hou Yifan. *DYLAN LOEB McCLAIN*

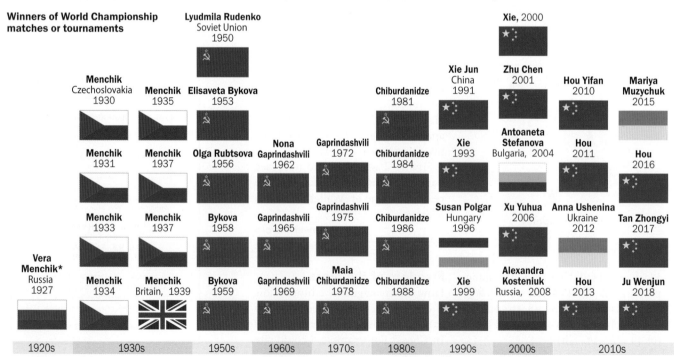

Winners of World Championship matches or tournaments

Vera Menchik*
Russia
1927

Menchik
Czechoslovakia
1930

Menchik
1931

Menchik
1933

Menchik
1934

Menchik
1935

Menchik
1937

Menchik
1937

Menchik
Britain, 1939

Lyudmila Rudenko
Soviet Union
1950

Elisaveta Bykova
1953

Olga Rubtsova
1956

Bykova
1958

Bykova
1959

Nona Gaprindashvili
1962

Gaprindashvili
1965

Gaprindashvili
1969

Gaprindashvili
1972

Gaprindashvili
1975

Maia Chiburdanidze
1978

Chiburdanidze
1981

Chiburdanidze
1984

Chiburdanidze
1986

Chiburdanidze
1988

Xie Jun
China
1991

Xie
1993

Susan Polgar
Hungary
1996

Xie
1999

Xie, 2000

Zhu Chen
2001

Antoaneta Stefanova
Bulgaria, 2004

Xu Yuhua
2006

Alexandra Kosteniuk
Russia, 2008

Hou Yifan
2010

Hou
2011

Anna Ushenina
Ukraine
2012

Hou
2013

Mariya Muzychuk
2015

Hou
2016

Tan Zhongyi
2017

Ju Wenjun
2018

1920s	1930s	1950s	1960s	1970s	1980s	1990s	2000s	2010s

*Menchik, the first Women's World Champion, who fled Russia after the 1917 Revolution, ended up playing under three flags, including Russia, which no longer existed.

Fair & Square

Charles Krauthammer: 'Chess: It's like alcohol. It's a drug. I have to control it, or it could overwhelm me. I have a regular Monday night game at home, and I do play a little online.'
(The chess-loving, Pulitzer Prize-winning US political commentator, author and Washington Post columnist, who died on June 21st).

Boris Gelfand: 'Chess history is full of big mistakes made on move 41 or 42.'
(In his 2015 book, Positional Decision Making in Chess)

Lord Hennessy: 'The Middle East, in diplomatic terms, is like playing simultaneous chess on about a dozen boards: there's usually three of them on fire, with President Trump's most recent action regarding Iran lighting a fourth quite deliberately.'
(The UK's leading constitutional expert and crossbench peer, on the 5 May BBC2 Daily Politics)

Alex Dunne: 'No real man would eat quiche, quote from *Peer Gynt*, or play correspondence chess.'
(In his American Chess Journal No.3 review of correspondence player Stephan Gerzadowicz' 1992 book, 'Journal of a Chess Master')

Eduard Dyckhoff: 'Over-the-board chess is the favourite of mortals; correspondence chess is the favourite of the gods.'
(The German doctor of law and Bavarian Chess Champion, who was considered an important figure in the development of correspondence chess in the early 20th century)

Tim Rice: 'It's not the moves of the pieces but the people that interest me.' *(The famed lyricist, asked in 1986 by a journalist before the premiere of 'Chess: The Musical', just what attracted him to write a musical about the game of chess)*

Jonathan Pearce: 'This has become a chess match in the home town of Boris Spassky - remember him?'
(The BBC football commentator, as Russia played Egypt at Krestovsky Stadium, St Petersburg, in the second round of the World Cup Group A matches)

Garry Kasparov: 'I don't think you can say that Arkady Dvorkovich "decided" to run for FIDE President. He was probably told to do so. That's how things work in authoritarian regimes.'
(To Nigel Short during the live broadcast of the Your Next Move rapid/blitz tournament in Leuven)

Guillem Balague: 'Guardiola is a sponge, keen to learn from anyone from England rugby union coach Eddie Jones to chess grandmaster Garry Kasparov. Perhaps on some level he is making up for his lack of structured education.'
(In a major feature in April for bbc.com: 'Pep Guardiola: The Man City manager described as football's Che Guevara')

Mikhail Botvinnik: 'Everything is in a state of flux, and that includes the world of chess.'
(The prophetic patriarch, even before Trump, Brexit and now the upcoming FIDE presidential election)

Alex Yermolinsky: 'Generally speaking, most chess players are boring, self-centred, money-oriented, poorly educated overgrown adolescents I couldn't care less about. With some exceptions, that includes the Linares crowd and all of the world's top twenty.'

Guardian TV Guide: 'All the thrilling urgency of correspondence chess played by second-class post.'
(On the slow-moving plot to 'McMafia', the BBC's London-based Russian mafia TV drama)

Mark Dvoretsky: 'It is not possible to become a great player without having learned how to analyse deeply and accurately.'

Ernst Grünfeld: 'I never make a mistake in the opening.'
(The German arch hypermodernist, when asked why he never played 1.e4)

Bobby Fischer: 'Best by test.'
(On playing 1.e4)

Caruana again ahead of Carlsen

Challenger fights back to win Altibox Norway Chess

With superior play and full points against world number two Fabiano Caruana and last year's winner Levon Aronian, Magnus Carlsen seemed to be on course in the 6th edition of Altibox Norway Chess until a sudden loss against Wesley So threw a spanner in the works. The World Champion stalled and it was his upcoming Challenger who crowned a mighty comeback to claim Norway's finest. **SIMEN AGDESTEIN** reports.

'**N**ever was so much owed by so many to so few!' I know I should be careful with the comparison, but the famous war-time speech by Winston Churchill referring to the brave British Royal Air Force pilots who fought the Germans during the critical times of the *Blitzkrieg*, did pop up in my mind as I sat thinking about the 6th edition of Altibox Norway Chess, and the organization team that once again made it happen, consisting of Kjell Madland, Benedicte Westre Skog and Frode Sømme.

Kjell has been the brain and the power behind this fantastic event ever since the first tournament in 2013. Magnus Carlsen hadn't yet become World Champion, with all the implications of his title for chess in Norway. Still, Kjell managed to recognize the potential and pushed through the idea of staging the world's strongest tournament in Norway. Frode has also been on the team right from the start and takes care of the IT-solutions. Benedicte got involved in 2014, and soon after she started working full-time with Norway Chess as the one and

only organizer who is actually getting paid. 'I love my job,' she says.

After following everything closely for two weeks as a commentator for the international broadcast, I became increasingly aware of the fact that there is a very small group of people doing an enormous amount of work. But there's also a group of wonderful volunteers from the two local chess clubs, Stavanger and Sandnes, who play an essential part in the logistics, for instance driving the players around in the now famous Norway Chess Mini's, and taking care of lots

With a clenched fist, Fabiano Caruana shows how pleased he is with his victory in Altibox Norway Chess, ahead of Magnus Carlsen, who he will challenge for the world title in November.

'Some started talking about an upcoming massacre when Magnus Carlsen beat Fabiano Caruana, first in the blitz and then again in the first round of the main event.'

of other practical matters for a lump sum to their clubs. I hereby gladly take the opportunity to praise them. Where would we be without them!

Stavanger is Norway's oil capital, and everything connected with the tournament has an air of class. On their arrival at the airport, the players could not fail to notice the big chess pieces with a personal welcome to each of them, before they were taken to their hotel in the cool black and white Mini's with the Altibox Norway Chess logo all over them. Each player was given a car, with or without a driver, for their entire stay. The organizers even bought two excellent bicycles for shared use. No effort was spared to make the players and their seconds have a good time. The prizes were equally generous, with 75,000

euros for the winner down to 12,000 euros for the bottom spot.

Altogether, there were 34 different 'events' during the tournament. There were press conferences, boat trips, an open international tournament, tournaments for kids, simuls, receptions for sponsors, and even a cooking competition with the players on one of the free days.

With about 150 guests, Norway Summit, a conference about artificial intelligence with internationally renowned speakers from all over the world, was the biggest side event. 'We want to capitalize on the chess tournament and the fact that the best chess players in the world are here,' Kjell explained, but it requires a big effort to make this project financially sustainable. I learnt that for the

moment, the tournament and everything that comes with it is not yet profitable, which increases my admiration for the organizers even more.

Taking too much for granted

Many years ago, after winning the Isle of Man tournament when it was much weaker than it is now, I had to give the winner's speech at the final ceremony. In my speech, I quoted something I believe Artur Jussupow had once said, that 'every chess player should once organize a tournament, because this would probably make them change their views on a few things'. With some shame I think back to the times when I was a young footballer and did not bother to show up at youth camps to sign autographs and meet the kids who were looking up to us. We just went to the shop and picked the best jogging shoes and let the club pay, taking so many things for granted.

Luckily, the calibre of today's chess elite is completely different. Kudos to all the players at Norway Chess for being great ambassadors for our sport! They played simuls, gave autographs, talked about their games with invaluable insight on the live broadcast and took part in the boat trip and especially the cooking competition with great enthusiasm. The big surprise was that Vishy Anand and Ding Liren actually won that one. The players were grouped together in pairs, and everyone thought Levon Aronian and Maxime Vachier-Lagrave would be the superior ones in the kitchen, but they struggled with the Hollandaise sauce.

Soon after the cooking event on the first free day, it actually transpired that Ding had broken his hip. He had fallen off his bike and must have suffered horribly during the cooking, but showed no signs of pain. The next day, Ding couldn't appear for his Round 4 game, because he had to undergo an operation. He wanted to continue the tournament, but the doctors said no, and so, unfortu-

Ding Liren displayed expert culinary skills in the cooking competition, but the next day it transpired that the Chinese number one had broken his hip and had to leave the tournament.

nately, he had to withdraw after three draws. His results were annulled and his remaining opponents were given an extra free day.

Ding's withdrawal was a big pity, but at least Shakhriyar Mamedyarov could play. Because at the start of the tournament it was the Azeri who seemed to be a serious candidate for withdrawal. Mamedyarov had arrived with a bad toothache and had to pay several visits to the dentist, but after a few days it seemed that the worst was over. However, his play was lacking in spirit. 'First I couldn't sleep, and now I sleep too much because of all the medication,' he said. This may explain some of his dry draws.

For the Norwegian press, the biggest story was the clash between the World Champion and his challenger in November, Fabiano Caruana. Some started talking about an upcoming massacre when Magnus Carlsen beat Fabiano Caruana, first in the preliminary blitz and then again in the first round of the main event.

Happy and rightfully contented organizers at the closing dinner: Benedicte Westre Skog, Frode Sømme and the driving force behind Norway Chess, Kjell Madland.

Magnus Carlsen
Fabiano Caruana
Stavanger 2018 (1)
Bishop's Opening

1.e4 e5 2.♗c4 ♘f6 3.d3 c6 4.♘f3 d5 5.♗b3 ♗b4+ 6.♗d2 ♗xd2+ 7.♘bxd2 a5
'A little unusual', Magnus mentioned after the game. 7...♗g4 and 7...♘bd7 seem to be the normal moves.

8.c3 ♘bd7 9.exd5 cxd5 10.0-0 0-0 11.♖e1 ♖e8 12.♘f1

I must admit that in the live broadcast we struggled to understand

Magnus's idea around here, but in hindsight I realize it's about making Black's bishop weak. White will play d4 at some point, which would kind of force ...e4, and then White will break with his f-pawn.

12...b5
As the only person present with supposed chess competence in the commentary room – in the first three days, the broadcast was led by Knut Skeie Solberg, a non-chess-playing journalist – I claimed over and over again that all Black's problems had started with this move. After 12...b6, Black would have had no worries, I said. After hearing Magnus explain

Stavanger blitz 2018		
1	Wesley So	6
2	Hikaru Nakamura	5½
3	Vishy Anand	5½
4	Magnus Carlsen	5
5	Shakhriyar Mamedyarov	4½
6	Maxime Vachier-Lagrave	4½
7	Fabiano Caruana	4½
8	Sergey Karjakin	3½
9	Levon Aronian	3
10	Ding Liren	3

things afterwards, I realized my understanding was very shallow. For me it was absolutely wonderful having the players come after the games to explain things, although I sometimes felt a bit stupid about the things I had said.

13.a4 b4 14.cxb4 axb4 15.♘e3 ♗b7 16.d4
The thematic break, which reduces Black's bishop to a sad wreck obstructed by the central pawns.

16...e4

17.♘e5!? We looked at 17.♘h4 g6 18.g3, with the idea of playing the knight to f4, but Magnus seemed to consider only 17.♘d2 and f3, or perhaps ♗c2 and ♘b3 as the alternative. The text-move is truer to his style.

17...♘xe5 18.dxe5 ♖xe5 19.♕d4

Here we, or rather I, were absolutely convinced that Magnus had a great position. The judgements changed quickly. In general, it was easy to take the side of the player who'd just moved.

19...♖e7 20.♖ac1 ♖d7

Now I wasn't so sure anymore, because it actually dawned on us that is was hard for White to make progress. Black's idea is to be ready for ...d4, when White takes on b4.

21.♖ed1 h6 22.♖c5 ♖a5 23.♖xa5 ♕xa5 24.h3 ♔h7 25.♖c1

25...♖c7??

'Just a blunder', according to Magnus. He thought the position was balanced if Black defended passively. Black's b-pawn surely is weak, but White cannot easily take it without unleashing the big potential of the black pieces. The moment White plays ♘c2, Black can send his knight to e6 with great prospects.

26.♖xc7 ♕xc7 27.♕xb4 ♕c1+ 28.♗d1

I was struggling to understand what was wrong with 28.♔h2. Magnus showed a line afterwards that wasn't totally convincing, but according to the computer, Magnus's choice was the best one.

28...♗a6 29.♕d4 ♗e2 30.♔h2 ♗xd1 31.♘xd1 ♕c7+ 32.♔g1 ♕c1 33.b4

White has won back the pawn and can just run with his queenside pawns, while Black is still struggling with the passive knight on f6.

33...e3 A desperate attempt that seemed to be doomed to fail, especially since Caruana was getting into serious time-trouble.

34.fxe3 ♘e4 35.♕xd5!

Magnus had the time to think and quickly found there was no danger.

35...♘d2 36.♕f5+

To go to e2 via d3 was also possible.

36...♔h8 37.♕g4 f5 38.♕e2 ♘e4

I felt big distress from my co-commentator around here, because I was totally engrossed in the analysis of Hikaru Nakamura and Ding Liren and their game and totally missed that Magnus and Caruana were nearing the climax in their game. But now, finally, we had switched over to the ongoing game. Nakamura instantly pointed out White's next move.

39.♕e1! ♕a1 40.a5

Everything is covered and Magnus is just two pawns up.

40...♘d6 41.♕d2 ♘c4 42.♕d4 ♕c1

43.♔f1

Magnus said afterwards that he may not have played the endgame in the most accurate way, but it doesn't matter. The following queen ending is easily winning.

43...♘xe3+ 44.♕xe3 ♕xd1+ 45.♔f2 ♕c2+ 46.♔g3 g5 47.♕e5+ ♔h7 48.♔h2 f4 49.♕d5 ♕a4 50.♕f7+ ♔h8 51.♕g6 ♕xb4 52.♕xh6+ ♔g8 53.♕xg5+ ♔h7

We were wondering why Caruana didn't just resign here and instead let himself be tortured for another hour or so. 'He had every right to do it; I would have done the same.' Magnus said. To us, it just seemed to emphasize Caruana's position as the underdog. But it gave us an excellent chance to hear a little bit of my co-commentator's view on the chess world. Knut is not a complete novice. He had also appeared in this role during the Carlsen-Karjakin match in New York, when Agon were seeking a journalist to lead the official broadcast and looked to Norway, since we actually are in the forefront of making chess popular on TV. Knut Solberg Skeie got the job

For the fourth tournament in a row, Magnus Carlsen and Fabiano Caruana met in the very first round. The World Champion won, but it's anyone's guess what this result says about their upcoming match.

and followed the whole thing with Judit Polgar as his chess expert. It's certainly interesting to hear his point of view on how to popularize chess on TV. I found it absolute wonderful to go through the games with the players, but does that make good TV? I presume most of our followers were chess players, and hopefully they also liked to listen to the players more than to us, but it's good to reflect a bit on what works on TV and what doesn't.

54.♕h5+ ♔g7 55.♕g5+ ♔h7 56.h4 ♕d6 57.♕h5+ ♔g7 58.♕g5+ ♔h7 59.h5 f3+ 60.g3 f2 61.♕g6+ ♔h8 62.♕xd6 f1♕ 63.♕h6+ ♔g8 64.♕e6+ ♔h8 65.♕e3 ♕b5 66.♕c3+ ♔h7 67.g4 ♕d5 68.♕c7+ ♔g8 69.♔g3 ♕e6 70.♕d8+ ♔h7 71.♕d3+ ♔h8 72.a6 ♕e5+ 73.♔h3 ♕a1 74.♕d8+ ♔h7 75.♕e7+ ♔h6 76.♕e3+ ♔h7 77.a7

And finally Caruana resigned.

After the game had finished, we started talking about the implications this result could have for the upcoming world championship match. 'A match is playing against

one man, and this is like leading 1-0,' we babbled. The players, however, claimed it didn't play any role. By coincidence, Carlsen and Caruana had also met in the first rounds of the previous three tournaments they played in together, London, Tata Steel and Grenke. In Wijk aan Zee, Magnus won the Tata Masters with a plus-5 score, while Caruana finished in the bottom part of the standings with minus-3. In the most recent of these three events, in Baden-Baden (Grenke), and now again in Stavanger, Caruana (despite losing his first-round game) finished first ahead of Magnus. It's not so obvious who's got a grip on whom. But it does seem to be clear that, come November, the world's two uncontested best players will fight for the World Championship, which hasn't happened since the encounters between Kasparov and Karpov in the 1980s.

When, following his win against Caruana, Magnus also beat Levon Aronian in Round 3, everyone thought the top seed was in cruise control and that he would win easily. Here is his second win, with notes by his second Peter Heine Nielsen.

NOTES BY
Peter Heine Nielsen

Magnus Carlsen
Levon Aronian
Stavanger 2018 (3)
Ruy Lopez, Berlin Defence

1.e4 e5 2.♘f3 In Round 1, Magnus had won a good game against Fabiano Caruana with 2.♗c4, but at top level that move is almost exclusively seen as an anti-Petroff move order.

2...♘c6 3.♗b5 ♘f6!?

4.0-0 In the first round, the game Anand-Aronian saw 4.d3 ♗c5 5.c3 d5 6.♘bd2 0-0 7.0-0 ♖e8 8.exd5 a6!. With 8...a6!, Aronian not only sprung an excellent opening novelty, but also managed to amuse the Norwegian audience in the confession booth by saying that he forgot to play ...a6 at move 3, and now seemed a good moment to correct the mistake! Even so, his switch from the Marshall to the Berlin seemed more than just a fling.

4...♘xe4 5.♖e1

The most solid of lines, that actually suited Magnus well as he was the sole leader at this point.

5...♘d6 6.♘xe5 ♗e7 7.♗f1 ♘xe5 8.♖xe5 0-0 9.d4 ♗f6 10.♖e1

By far the main move, but in the 2016 New York World Championship match vs. Karjakin, Magnus put the rook on e2 – an idea of Caruana's second Kasimdzhanov – and had some pressure before the game was eventually drawn.

10...♘f5!?

Also the latest trend. Black used to go 10...♖e8, and while that still makes a solid impression, the preference of the experts has shifted to this slightly more aggressive move.

11.d5 Grabbing space, or, from Black's perspective, slightly weakening White's pawn chain. Less ambitious and a bit more solid is 11.c3 d5, with numerous games being drawn shortly after.

11...♖e8 In reply to this, everybody routinely played the standard move 12.♘d2 until Caruana tried 12.♗d3 against Aronian in Baden-Baden this year. Magnus's next move was intended to be a novelty.

12.♖xe8+!? But to my surprise this had already been played by Palac in 2005, against me! The unimpressive continuation was 12...♕xe8 13.♘d2 d6, and a draw was agreed.

12...♕xe8

13.♕d3!? Putting the bishop on d3, similar to what Caruana did, looks like a normal move. The text-move runs somewhat counter to general chess principles: developing your queen first and then figuring out how to proceed next is not exactly what is recommended in beginners' books. But apart from the primitive threat of taking the knight on f5, this move supports the e4-square, to which the white knight is due to be transferred, because it generally would have much more scope there. Aronian seemed surprised, but after some thought played the obvious reply:

13...d6 14.♘d2

Intending ♘e4, followed by c3, ♗d2 and ♖e1. The good thing about White's position is that it has a lot of room for improvement! For Black it's more difficult. Probably, especially as White is not fully developed, 14...c6!?, switching to an isolani type of position after White takes dxc6 or Black takes ...cxd5, would assure Black counterplay. But Black has an almost perfect pawnstructure, so voluntarily ruining it is not an easy over-the-board decision.

14...♗g5?!

After his win against Levon Aronian, Magnus Carlsen joined Simen Agdestein and Knut Solberg Skeie in the studio of the international live broadcast.

♗xc6 Black obviously is slightly worse, but in a less suffocating way than in the game.

20...a5 21.a4 Now 21...c5 would leave the b5-square weak, thus he should have continued 21...c6!.

21...♘e8

A very logical move, assuring the exchange of the dark-squared bishops and at the same time eliminating the ♘e4 threat.

15.♘f3

A case (the engines!) could be made for including g3 and h4 in order to gain a bit of time, but Magnus either wanted to assure himself of the following favourable exchanges, or perhaps, as becomes relevant further on in the game, not lose the flexibility of his kingside pawns.

15...♗xc1 16.♖xc1 ♗d7 17.♖e1

At first sight it looks like a typical quick ♖e1 Berlin draw is in the making. Rooks will be exchanged on the e-file and White can do absolutely nothing constructive with his moderate space advantage. But details do matter! After 17...♕f8 White will immediately attack

Black's queenside with a move like 18.♕b3 or 18.♕c4, when Black is reduced to a passive defence, using his rook to defend the weakness on c7. This may seem a small nuance, but it has a huge effect. Black has no way of making the necessary exchanges and is doomed to passivity. His position is so solid that the chances of him succeeding to hang on are obviously there, but White's edge, as indicated by the engines, is certainly larger than it looks.

17...♕d8 18.♕c4 g6 19.h3 ♘g7 20.♖e3

A nice set-up. The rook might be used to attack the vulnerable spots on the queenside or, more directly, on the kingside, as happened in the game. It did, however, give Aronian the chance to switch to a pawn structure with an isolani. After 20...c5! 21.dxc6

22.♕d4 An ideal square for the queen. Normally speaking, 22...♕f6 would chase it away, but with the black g-pawn on g6, White has the small tactic 23.♖xe8+!, which means that Black will never achieve a ♕f6+♔g7 set-up.

22...♘g7 23.g4!?

Logical and strong. Magnus controls the f5-square, not allowing ...♘f5, attacking his queen. The weakening of his own king is not a concern in view of Black's passivity. Even so, the engines seem to think that White should have increased his edge with the less compromising 23.♗d3.

23...c6

At last, and with the logical justification that White's last move has turned the battle from a positional into a tactical one, Aronian stops caring about his pawn structure and tries to create counterplay.

23...♕f8, intending 24...♖e8, looks solid and logical, but then 24.♘g5! becomes alarming, since 24...♖e8 is met by 25.♘e4!, creating access to the f6-square, with immediate disaster for Black. Suffice it to say that the engines suggest 24...♕d8!.

24.c4

24...♘e8

With all this suffering, why not at least have a pawn for it? 24...c5 25.♕f4 ♗xa4 was possible, when White has excellent compensation in numerous ways. The engines prefer 26.♖a3!? ♗d7 27.♖b3, eyeing the b6-square!

25.♕f4 ♔g7

Adding to his misery, Levon was also desperately short of time. Magnus now pulls off an almost basketball-like trick, first looking to one side, then attacking fiercely on the other.

26.♖b3 Just a decoy.

26...♖b8 27.♘g5!

27...♘f6? 27...♕f6 still holds on. While 28.♕d2 attacks the a5-pawn, Black can defend with 28...h6 29.♘e4 ♕d8 without facing disaster. Now, however, swift tactics decide.

28.♖f3!

28...h6 Not even a blunder, seeing that Black has no meaningful defence left anyway. The d6-pawn

is under attack and 28...♕e7 29.♖e3 ♕f8 leaves White with so many options that the engines do not even mention that 30.♕xf6+?!, followed by 31.♘xh7+, wins a pawn, simply because the easiest win is 30.♕d4!, with a crushing pin.

29.♘e4! ♘xe4 30.♕xf7+ ♔h8 31.♕xg6

And facing the combined threats to the e4-knight and the h6-pawn, as well as ♖f7, mating, Aronian resigned.

■ ■ ■

After his impressive start, Magnus somehow didn't manage to follow up, and when he surprisingly lost to Wesley So in Round 6, the tension was back again. It was the first time ever that So defeated the World Champion in a classical game.

NOTES BY
Wesley So

Wesley So
Magnus Carlsen
Stavanger 2018 (6)
Slav Defence, Exchange Variation

People like to say that I don't play my best against Carlsen. Don't think I hadn't noticed that, but it took my dad Renato to explain it to me. He told me it's like being a very young and talented soccer player and having pictures of Pele all over your room and knowing every game he ever played by heart. You think about him, dream about him, grow up wanting to be as good as him and when playing by yourself even pretend you *are* him. And then one day Pele suddenly appears on the field. You can't move. You can't breathe. Everything is a blur. Which goal posts are yours? You feel like you might faint. Or die. You are overwhelmed because he is older, bigger and has years of experience on you. You see that you are a kid with over-size dreams.

Playing Carlsen in Norway is probably like playing Pele in Brazil. It has good points in that the focus is always on him and no one really cares about your games unless you lose to him. You can be sure of a dismissive attitude from the Norwegian commentators and a local audience who only came to see one player (who is that brown boy anyway?).

I appreciate this because it's very freeing not to carry the burden of expectation. It allows me to focus on the excellence of the Altibox Norway Chess experience (which is one of the best organized events in Europe – a professional chess player's dream tournament).

I really love Stavanger, and after a meal of my favourite food (salmon) I went to play my game against the favoured son of Norway, whom in my 3½ years of professional play I had never beaten in a classical game.

1.d4

Considering how well-prepared Magnus is in the opening these days, I decided to stick to normal lines and not challenge him on the intricacies of the Ruy Lopez.

1...d5 2.c4 c6 3.cxd5

3.♘f3 ♘f6 4.e3 is usually how my games against Magnus go. I've had this position against him with both colours.

3...cxd5 Apparently, the commentators announced I was playing for a draw by taking on d5... A shocking analysis, as we'd only traded one pawn!

4.♗f4

4...♘f6 I thought he'd start with 4...♘c6 5.♘c3, and now he has the extra option of 5...e5!? (5...♗f5 6.e4!?).

5.♘c3 ♘c6 6.♘f3

6...a6 I had expected 6...♘h5 7.♗d2 ♘f6, which seems to be the most solid variation, but Magnus went for the sub-line.

6...♗f5 7.e3 e6 8.♕b3 ♗b4 9.♘e5 has become very fashionable lately. Yaroslav Zherebukh beat Ray Robson with it in the US Championship just a couple of months ago.

7.♖c1 ♗f5 8.e3 I had a little experience with this variation, having played it against Ivanchuk almost a decade ago, when I was 13!

> '**And then one day Pele suddenly appears on the field. You can't move. You can't breathe. Everything is a blur. Which goal posts are yours?**'

8...♖c8

8...e6 9.♕b3 ♖a7 is how my game against Ivanchuk went in the 2009 World Cup.

9.♗e2 e6 10.0-0

10...♘d7 He played this quite fast, so I assumed he was still following his opening ideas.

10...♗e7 11.♕b3! ♘a5 12.♕a4+ is supposed to be better for White due to 12...♘c6 13.♗xa6!.

10...♗d6 11.♗xd6 ♕xd6 12.♘a4 is not a nice position for Black. Normally, he wouldn't want to trade his dark-squared bishop in the Exchange Slav.

11.♘a4 ♗e7

This quietly threatens an attack on the kingside with ...g5/...h5.

12.h3

A prophylaxis against the aforementioned idea.

After a meal of his favourite food (salmon), Wesley So went to play his game against 'the favourite son of Norway'. And you can see from his mood afterwards how that game went!

16...♞xa3?!
White would be clearly better after 16...b6 17.♗xc4 dxc4 18.♕xd8 ♗xd8 19.♗d6.
With hindsight, 16...b5! bolsters the knight, and it might be the best defence: 17.a4 ♞b2 18.♕d2 ♞xa4 19.♞d4 ♗g6, and this is very unclear. White has compensation for the pawn, but perhaps not much more.
17.♞d4 ♗e4 18.f3 ♗g6 19.♕b3
I wasn't really worried about sacrificing the a-pawn, since his knight is side-lined in many lines.
19...♞c4 20.♗xc4 dxc4 21.♕xc4

21...♕e8!?
An interesting option, and one I could hardly have expected. Black keeps the bishop pair for now and wants to kick my knight away from its central outpost by making the ...e6-e5 break work.
I thought he would go for 21...♗g5, which is the most natural move, and now 22.♗xg5 ♕xg5, since I am slightly better (but not much more). In fact, I couldn't see anything clear during the game. My dark squares are a little vulnerable and Black is ready to fight for control of the d-file. 23.♕c3 is what I was thinking of

12...0-0
Magnus castles quite early.
Apparently, 12...g5!? is still very good here. I won't give it an exclamation mark, since the position remains very unclear, but it is definitely a good alternative: 13.♗h2 h5. Now the kingside pawns look threatening. The position is quite weird and analysis shows it's not easy to play for both sides: 14.♞d2 (14.♞e1 g4 15.♗d3 ♗xd3 16.♞xd3 ♖g8 17.♔h1, unclear) 14...g4 15.hxg4 hxg4 16.♗xg4 ♗d3! 17.♗e2 ♗b4! 18.♞f3 ♗e4, with

chances for both sides.
13.a3 Preparing to push my pawns forward. White is simply faster and better equipped to seize the initiative on the queenside.

13...♞a5
13...b5 14.♞c5 ♞xc5 15.dxc5 ♗f6 16.♞d4 ♗xd4 17.exd4 ♕f6 18.♗e3 e5 19.dxe5 ♕xe5 20.♕d2 is a long forcing line that favours White.
14.♞c5! ♞c4 15.b4 ♞xc5 16.dxc5
And not 16.bxc5 b6, with equality.

playing, and then 23...♖fd8 24.♖fd1 h5 25.♘b3 ♗f5 26.♔h1! ♕g3 27.♕e1, and with a few accurate moves White will manage to keep a nagging edge. Over the board, however, the position is never really crystal-clear.

22.♗g3

Just a calm non-committal move, because I couldn't find anything definitive. I decided to just make a move and see what Magnus intended to do next.

22.c6!? e5! (22...b5 23.♕c3 is just winning for White; the c-pawn is simply too strong) 23.♗xe5 bxc6 24.♘xc6 ♗xb4 was the line that Magnus had calculated. Black holds here.

22.e4 e5 23.♗xe5 ♗xc5 24.bxc5 ♕xe5 is better for White, as the bishop on g6 is buried for the time being, but I think Black can hold here, too.

22...e5

22...♗g5 was better: 23.♖fe1 ♕d7, and it is not so easy to break down Black's defences.

23.♘b3

23...♗d8? This just blunders a pawn. Magnus missed 26.♗d6 in the variation below (see the comment to Black's 25th move).

23...e4 is an option, but I suppose he wasn't attracted to it because of 24.f4 ♗f5 25.♘d4 ♗d7 26.f5, with a clear white advantage.

23...♗f5 also does not fully equalize: 24.♗xe5 ♗e6 25.♕c3 ♗xb3 26.♕xb3 ♗xc5 27.♖xc5 ♖xc5 28.♗xg7!, with attacking chances.

The best defence was 23...h6!, but over the board this is hard to see.

24.♕d5 Grabbing the gift.

24...♕b5?! Another mistake.

24...♗c7 is perhaps a better defence, e.g. 25.♘a5 ♗xa5 26.bxa5 ♕e7 27.♕xe5 ♕xe5 28.♗xe5 ♗d3 29.♖fd1 ♗b5 and White is a clear pawn up. But the opposite-coloured bishops give Black good chances to hold. I would estimate Black's drawing chances at 30 to 40%.

25.♗xe5

25...♗e7 25...♕xb4 26.♗d6 is what he had overlooked.

26.♕d2 I consolidate the pawn, of course. I was really delighted with my position here.

26.♘a5! b6 27.♘b7 is the computer's fastest way to destroy any Black resistance. Suffice it to say that I did not even see 27.♘b7 during the game.

26...♖fd8 27.♗d6 ♗f6 28.e4 h6

White is definitely winning now. The only question is how to convert my advantage. Having a winning position does not mean a thing unless you can carefully nurse your advantage to a win. As a famous player once pointed out: 'Anyone can get an advantage, but only the best players convert them.'

29.♘d4 ♗xd4+ 30.♕xd4 ♖e8

Trading pawns does not help at all: 30...a5 31.bxa5 ♕xa5 32.♖a1, when the b7-pawn is going to fall.

31.♖fe1 ♔h7

32.g4! We were already quite short on time here, which is why I didn't hesitate to attack!

32.f4 f5 is what I wanted to prevent. The last thing we want is for Black to have some sort of light-square blockade.

32...f6 33.f4

33...♕c6?

After this blunder Black should be totally lost.

33...♗f7 is clearly a better defence. The queen is just better placed on b5:

34.f5 a5 35.bxa5 ♖a8, and if Black manages to activate a rook along the a-file he has some saving chances.

34.f5 ♗f7 35.h4

Here I knew for a fact that I was winning. However, converting advantages is never easy, as you can see from past games. For example, there is a famous Magnus game from 2014; a 4.f3 Nimzo. His opponent was totally winning for many moves, even getting to (computer evaluation) +15 at some

point, but he managed to find all the worst moves and ended up losing.

35...♖a8 36.♖c2

36.♖c3 was my first intention, which would have been very strong. I rejected it because of 36...a5 37.g5 axb4 (37...♗h5 38.♖g3 and compared with the rook on g2 there is a big difference: Black has no 38...♗f3! counterplay) 38.g6+ ♗xg6 39.fxg6+ ♔xg6, and Black has two pawns but hey, a piece is a piece!

36...a5 37.g5

37...♗h5!

A very good sneaky last try, and one which I underestimated.

38.g6+

In Norway there is no time increment or delay until move 60, so time-trouble is definitely an issue. Here I used up all my time calculating until I found a series of moves that would safely take me to move 40.

I was hesitant to open the g-file, but simplest is 38.gxf6 gxf6 39.b5! (a very important move, closing the a-file and opening the b-file for White) 39...♕xb5 40.♖b2 ♕d7 41.♕xf6 ♖g8+ 42.♔h2, when Black has absolutely no counterplay.

38...♔h8 39.b5! ♕xb5 40.♖b2

'When they told me, I burst out laughing because, after all, so what? Sometimes I do make boring draws. Sometimes.'

40...♕c6?

Magnus used up almost all of his remaining time and made another mistake. This makes the game very easy to convert.

40...♕d7 would have made the game harder for me, but, as my friend Anish Giri pointed out, White still wins easily with the right moves:

ANALYSIS DIAGRAM

41.♕d5! (41.♖eb1 ♗f3 42.♖xb7 ♕c6 43.e5 ♕c8! is what I had missed in my calculations back on move 37) 41...♕c6 42.♕d3 a4 43.♖b6 ♕c8 44.♕d5!. White just plays the same position a tempo down, as in the game. No worries. 44...a3 (44...♖a7 45.♕f7! a3 46.c6 a2 47.♖xb7 winning) 45.♖xb7 ♖g8 (45...a2 46.♖xg7) 46.c6 a2 47.♖a1, and White wins.

41.♖b6 ♕c8 42.♕d5

42...a4

42...♖a7 43.♕f7 threatens 44.c6 and

wins. Due to back-rank issues, Black's counterplay comes way too late: 43...♗f3 44.c6 ♖xe4 45.♖xe4 ♗xe4 46.♗f8, and mate on the next move.

43.♖xb7 ♖g8

43...♗xg6 44.fxg6 ♕g4+ 45.♔f2 does not do much either, since I have ♗g3 to counter his check on h4.

44.c6

Threatening 45.c7 and 46.♖b8, which is why Magnus finally resigned!

This was a big win for me, being my first victory against him in classical chess, and it also evened up the standings in the tournament, since we were now co-leaders with +1, and with only three games to go.

44.♖c7 ♕e8 45.♕d2 a3? 46.♕xh6+!! was another way to win.

In the after-game interview, Ian Rogers asked me if I had played with special focus because I was provoked by a statement my opponent made before the game. It seems he had said that I am a player who makes boring draws and he could draw me at will. Actually, having no interest in social media, I was completely unaware of these comments.

When they told me, I burst out laughing because, after all, so what? Sometimes I do make boring draws. Sometimes.

■ ■ ■

The final rounds were tense and tight. Going into the last round, four players were tied for first: Carlsen and all three Americans: Caruana, Nakamura and So. A play-off seemed far from unlikely. If two players shared first place, a blitz play-off would be held immediately after the last round. If more players tied for first place, the play-off would take place the next day.

A bit surprisingly, Carlsen drew quickly with Maxime Vachier-Lagrave, and Nakamura did the same against Levon Aronian. Now a multiple playoff would follow if Caruana and So also drew their game. In the meantime, Anand joined the 'leaders' at plus-one when Karjakin suddenly blundered.

When Vishy Anand beat Sergey Karjakin in the last round, suddenly a five-way play-off loomed… Anand confessed that he was not too optimistic this chance would materialize and he was right.

Sergey Karjakin
Vishy Anand
Stavanger 2018 (9)
Queen's Gambit Declined

1.d4 ♘f6 2.c4 e6 3.♘f3 d5 4.♘c3 ♗e7 5.♗f4 0-0 6.e3 c5 7.dxc5 ♗xc5 8.♕c2 ♘c6 9.a3 ♕a5 10.0-0-0

10.♖d1 would transpose to Aronian-Nakamura on the neighbouring board.

10...♘e4 As an amateur I wondered what would happen if White took twice on e4, but the computer shows immediately that Black will draw by taking on a3.

11.♘b5 a6 12.♘c7 e5 13.♖xd5

Kasparov played this for the first time against Vaganian back in 1992. Now it's all computer analysis, but the problem here for me is that my computer shows a white advantage, making me realize that there is a significant difference in strength between computers and especially the software they are running on. Nakamura said in the commentator room that it was no secret that all top players are connected to far stronger machines back home. An ordinary laptop is not good enough.

13...exf4

Vaganian played 13...f5, but the exchange sacrifice 14.♖xe5! was good for White.

14.♕xe4 ♕xc7 15.♖xc5 fxe3 16.♗d3 g6 17.fxe3 ♗e6 18.♕h4

Obviously, this was all computer analysis, especially on Karjakin's side, but it confused us that our computer said Black was slightly

better after 18...♕d6. Why would Karjakin go for something that's just worse for him? Karjakin confirmed what we saw: that after 19.♕h6 ♕xc5 20.♘g5 ♕xe3+ 21.♔b1 ♖fd8 (or somewhere) Black is not mated. He showed 19.♘g5 h5 20.♕e4, when my computer still gives Black the edge. After blitzing until here, Anand stopped for a long think and played something else.

18...♖ae8 19.♗e4 ♕b6 20.♕h6

In the studio, both Aronian and Nakamura seemed to like Black after 20...♕xc5 21.♘g5 ♕xe3+ 22.♔b1 ♕xg5 23.♕xg5 ♗xc4, but Karjakin, like the computer, believed that only White could be better here.

20...f5 21.♘g5

21...♖f7!
The only move, but a cool one.
22.♗d5
There's a lot to think about here, but both players seem to find the best path out of the mess.
22...♗xd5 23.♖xd5 ♕xe3+
24.♔b1 ♖fe7 25.♖hd1 ♕e2

26.h4??
26.♖d6, followed by taking on g6 and a perpetual, would be the logical

outcome of the game. Karjakin must have thought that Black's reply was not possible.
26...♘e5!
Anand didn't spend much time on this one. The point is that 27.♖d8 would win but for 27...♕xd1+! 28.♖xd1 ♘g4, and the queen is trapped.
27.♘f3 ♕e4+

Black has many good options here, and Anand thought he didn't play totally accurately, but it was surely good enough.
28.♔a2 ♕xc4+ 29.♔a1 ♘g4
30.♕c1 ♕xc1+ 31.♖xc1 ♔g7
32.h5?
Another blunder, which doesn't change the result, but says something about Karjakin's form at the end.
32...♘f6 0-1.

Now all the attention turned to the final game between Caruana and So. Would it be a draw and result in a five-way play-off? We join them in the critical phase.

Fabiano Caruana
Wesley So
Stavanger 2018 (9)

position after 30.♖bc1

Anand said afterwards that he was not optimistic about a playoff around here, since there was an '80 per cent chance that someone would win this position'.
30...gxf3 I thought it was stupid to hand the long diagonal to White, and was a bit surprised to hear afterwards that Caruana felt he was slightly better here. After 30...♔b8 he was ready for 31.b6, and perhaps Black's weaknesses were worse than White's.

31.♕xf3 ♖ed8
So had about 10 minutes left here, while Caruana was down to a minute or so for the remaining eight moves. The time-limit was 100 minutes for the first 40 moves with no increments, so a good old-fashioned time-scramble was looming.
32.♗c4 Caruana discounted 32.a6 ♖xd3 33.♕xb7+ ♕xb7 34.axb7 ♔xb7 35.♗xf7 ♔b6 after perhaps two seconds of thought, and just protected the d-pawn instead.

32...e4?
Perhaps, So wanted to mess it up in Caruana's time-trouble, but the positional compensation he gets is not worth a pawn, and certainly not two.
33.dxe4 ♕e5 34.♗xf7!
Caruana didn't believe in Black's concept and instantly took the second pawn as well.
34...♖d3 35.♗f2 ♖8d4 36.♗d5

Here, So suddenly stopped for a long think, which revealed that he did *not* have control. Perhaps his original intention was 36...♘g4 37.♕h4 ♖h3, which is a cool line. White can't take the rook, either with the pawn or the queen, without being mated, but White comes first after taking on c5, and mates on d8 if the king goes to b8, or alternatively gives a bishop check on e6 and takes the queen in case of ...♔d7.
36...♔d7 37.b6?!
37.♖xc5, with the threat of 38.♗e6+, is obvious and good, but Caruana said he was worried about his back rank.
37...axb6 38.axb6 ♘g4

39.♕g1!
Now 39.♕h4 ♖h3 would work, but White could simply slide back and defend.
39...♔d8
After 39...♖d2 40.♖f1 Black can't fuel up the attack.

40.h3??
Caruana actually had 27 seconds left on the clock, but still made this big blunder fairly quickly, because he had seen the line that happened in the game.
40...♖xh3+
So's clock was also ticking down to zero. He found the right move, but not the reasoning behind it.
41.gxh3

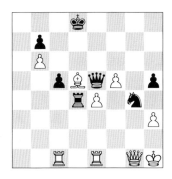

41...♖d3??

So returned the favour and, even worse, did so after only three seconds. After 41...♖d2! it's actually a draw by force after 42.hxg4 hxg4 43.♕g2 (the only move that prevents mate) 43...♕h8+ 44.♔g1 ♖xg2+ 45.♔xg2 ♕h3+, and a perpetual. A terrible finish for So, who made many new fans during this tournament. On the first day, he played a simul in a shopping mall against local players. He won the preliminary blitz tournament (which again served as the drawing of lots) and just hours after this terrible blow he was wearing the same big smile again and played another simul against the sponsors. Actually, he was in big trouble against a 1500-player and pretended to be mightily relieved when he made a draw.

42.♕g2

Now it's hopelessly lost for Black.

42...♖g3 43.hxg4 ♖xg2 44.♔xg2 h4 45.♔f3! The king just 'goes for a walk', as Anand put it.

45...♕g3+ 46.♔e2 h3 47.♖g1 ♕h4 48.e5 1-0.

After 48...h2 49.♖gd1 Black can't even take on g4 due to 50.♗f3+, and then 'it's not possible to blunder', Caruana said.

And that's what you do when it's all over: have a cocktail and play blitz. As Caruana and MVL unwind, Nakamura seems to be itching to join the fun.

Caruana's win was greeted with great applause from everyone present, including the Norwegians. The American's victory was highly deserved. He was the biggest fighter in the tournament and a very popular winner. The Norwegians are mad about Magnus Carlsen, but they also appreciate worthy opposition. Sergey Karjakin (and even his manager) gained many supporters during the World Championship match in New York two years ago, and I'm sure Caruana will do the same in London in November, no matter the result.

Caruana was also clearly the most social player in the field. Literally every evening, he and his second Rustam Kasimdzhanov were playing Avalon in the hotel lobby with whoever wanted to join them. I did once and thought this was a great way to get to know the best chess players in the world a bit better!

The transformation from a horrible start to actually winning the whole thing is also something the audience appreciates. Caruana had lost to Anish Giri in the German Bundesliga playoff just days before the tournament, did not impress at all in the preliminary blitz and lost his first

game against Magnus. But he rose from the ashes and came out on top. What a World Championship match to look forward to!

The turnaround for Caruana came with the following win in Round 4.

Fabiano Caruana
Sergey Karjakin
Stavanger 2018 (5)
English Opening, Four Knights Variation

1.c4 ♘f6 2.♘c3 e5 3.♘f3 ♘c6 4.e3 ♗b4 5.♕c2 ♗xc3 6.♕xc3 ♕e7

7.b3!? The point, as Caruana explained, is 7...d5 8.d4 exd4 9.♘xd4 ♘xd4 10.♕xd4, and now White can take back with the bishop on c4 in one go, because White normally plays 7.♗e2.

7...0-0 8.♗b2 ♖e8 9.a3 a5 10.h3 b6

11.♗e2 I suggested 11.g4 in the commentary room and was a bit surprised that Mamedyarov, who was also there, actually thought the idea was interesting.
11...♗b7 12.0-0 d5 13.cxd5 ♘xd5 14.♕c2 e4 15.♘h2 ♕g5

16.f4 Perhaps 16.f3 was more precise, but after Black's reply it didn't matter.
16...exf3 17.♘xf3 ♕g3 18.♖f2 ♖ad8 19.♗c4

White is directing all his pieces towards the kingside and actually has a wonderful position, despite the slow opening. Karjakin's next move is either very good or a sign of desper-

ation and just very bad. As the game shows, it was probably the latter.
19...♘f6 20.♗xf6 gxf6 21.♖af1 ♖d6

22.b4! A surprise, even to the computers, but it seems to work.
22...axb4 23.axb4 ♖e7
The point is 23...♘xb4 24.♗xf7+ ♔xf7 25.♕xc7, and White gets the material back with interest, since 25...♖e7 is brilliantly refuted by 26.♘g5+!.
24.b5 ♘e5 25.♘d4 ♗c8 26.♔h1 ♔g7 27.♗e2

Black's position is absolutely dreadful. Karjakin can't do anything and Caruana has all the time in the world to improve his pieces.
27...♔h8 28.♕c3 ♔g7 29.♗d1 ♔g8 30.♗c2 ♕h4 31.♖f4 ♕g3 32.♗f5 ♗b7 33.♗e4 ♗c8

34.♕a3! Finally it's time for the queen to enter Black's position with devastating force.
34...♔g7 35.♕a8

35...♗xh3 With the clock ticking down to zero, Karjakin just goes for some revenge checks.
36.gxh3 ♕xh3+ 37.♔g1 ♖xd4 38.♗g2 ♕g3 39.♖xd4 ♘g4 40.♖f3 ♕e1+ 41.♗f1 1-0.
There's no perpetual here, especially since the queen can drop back to g2 if needed.

Caruana made the next step, to plus-1, in the penultimate round by beating Anand with an opening idea that he himself believed was just dubious.

Vishy Anand
Fabiano Caruana
Stavanger 2018 (8)
Petroff Defence

1.e4 e5 2.♘f3 ♘f6 3.♘xe5 d6 4.♘f3 ♘xe4 5.d3 ♘f6 6.d4 d5 7.♗d3 ♗d6 8.0-0 0-0 9.♗g5 h6 10.♗h4 ♘c6 11.c3 g5 12.♗g3 ♘e4 13.♗xd6 cxd6!?

What a curious structure!

14.♘fd2

I was wondering what Caruana had in mind against 14.♕b3, and surprisingly it seemed that he didn't have anything special. The lines he showed starting with 14...♗e6 15.♕xb7 didn't seem totally convincing.

14...f5 15.♘a3 ♗e6 16.♘c2 ♘xd2 17.♕xd2 f4 18.♖ae1 ♕f6 19.f3

Now only Black can be better, we thought, although the computer doesn't quite agree. It looks at the doubled d-pawns, I guess, but it's hard to find a plan for White, while Black is ready for a kingside attack.

19...♖f7 20.♖e2 ♖af8 21.♘e1 ♘e7 22.♗c2 a5 23.♗b3 ♖g7 24.♕d3 ♗d7 25.a4 ♔h8 26.♕d2 h5 27.♘d3

27...♘f5

Now it becomes very sharp!

28.♗xd5 ♘e3 29.♖xe3 fxe3 30.♕xe3 ♗xa4 31.♖a1 ♖e7 32.♕d2 ♗b5 33.♖xa5 ♗xd3 34.♕xd3 ♖e1+ 35.♔f2 ♖fe8

The character of the position has changed completely. Materially speaking, it's interesting, but Black's rooks are active.

36.♖a8

After the game Anand suggested 36.g3?, thinking he should hold, but Caruana was ready with 36...♕f5!, and White can resign, since it's mate on e2 if the queen is taken, and 37.♗e4 ♕xa5 38.♔xe1 d5 is a rook up for Black.

36...♕f4 37.♖xe8+ ♖xe8 38.♕d1 ♕xh2 39.♕d2 ♕h4+ 40.♔f1 ♕h1+ 41.♔f2 ♕h4+ 42.♔f1 ♖a8 43.♔e2 ♖a1 44.♔d3 b5 45.c4 bxc4+ 46.♔xc4 ♕f4

47.♕e2?

This doesn't work. Caruana agreed that the endgame after 47.♕xf4 gxf4 48.♗e6 didn't seem so clear, but he thought he was winning and backed it up with some convincing lines.

47...♕c1+ 48.♔b5 ♕c8!

This seals White's fate. Black's attack is far stronger than White's.

49.♔b6

49.♕e7 ♕a6 is mate in a few moves. 49.♔b4 seems to be the only move to prolong the game.

49...♕b8+ 50.♔c6 ♖c1+ 0-1.

51.♗c4 ♕c8+ 52.♔d5 ♖xc4! 53.♕xc4 ♕g8+ skewers the king and the queen.

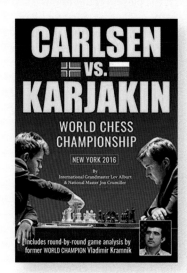

Overall, we saw some interesting games, but there are usually too many dry draws these days, and the same was the case in Stavanger. Obviously, it's not easy to win or just get something out of the opening against such well-prepared players, but it would be good if the players could find ways to satisfy the audience's thirst for blood, and pre-arranged draws or the suspicion of them certainly doesn't help either. Magnus Carlsen caused some upheaval when he said on Norwegian TV that he had no proof, but that he suspected that the following draw had been agreed on in advance.

Shakhriyar Mamedyarov
Sergey Karjakin
Stavanger 2018 (3)
Italian Game

1.e4 e5 2.♘f3 ♘c6 3.♗c4 ♗c5 4.c3 ♘f6 5.d3 d6 6.0-0 h6 7.♖e1 0-0 8.h3 a5

All this is actually very interesting. Karjakin explained afterwards that he had prepared this opening deeply before the Candidates tournament in Berlin and generously revealed many interesting ideas. Advancing the a-pawn two steps rather than one has become increasingly more common lately.

9.♘bd2 ♗e6 10.♗b5 ♕b8

A cool and fashionable idea.

11.♘f1 ♕a7 12.♖e2 a4 13.♘g3 ♕a5 14.♗xc6 bxc6 15.♘h4

To my great surprise, they were following a game of one of my students. Johan Salomon, the latest Norwegian GM, played this against

'Magnus Carlsen caused some upheaval when he said that he suspected that the draw had been agreed on in advance.'

Aleksej Aleksandrov at the Aeroflot Open just some months earlier.

15...♖fe8

Aleksandrov played 15...♔h7.

16.♖e1 ♔h7 17.♕f3 d5 18.exd5 ♗xd5 19.♕f5+

Commentating on the game, I was naively enthusiastic around here. 19...♔g8 20.♗xh6 seemed like a pawn for White, and coming up with the alternative was impossible without computer assistance.

19...g6

Of course, Karjakin had analysed everything. Mamedyarov is not a 1.e4-player, and one might think that he could not possibly have looked at a rare line like this in advance. But it's Black who is making the miraculous moves here. White's play is logical and seemingly extremely promising as well, which feels like an argument for the players' honesty.

20.♘xg6

After 20.♕xf6 ♗e7 21.♕xe5 ♗xh4

22.♕xe8 ♖xe8 23.♖xe8, 23...a3! was important, according to Karjakin's preparation.

20...fxg6 21.♕xf6 ♖f8 22.♕h4

22...g5!! This is the star move in the line, and one that my computer doesn't find until you actually make it. After 22...♖xf2 23.♕xh6+ ♔g8 24.♘e4 the queen is protected by the g-pawn and there is no dangerous discovered check.

23.♗xg5 ♖xf2 24.♕xh6+ ♔g8 25.♕g6+ ♔h8 26.♕h6+

The final point is 26.♕h5+ ♔g8 27.♘e4 ♗f7!, and there is no safe square for the queen.

ANALYSIS DIAGRAM

26...♔g8 27.♕g6+ ♔h8 28.♕h6+ ½-½.

Certainly an entertaining draw, but did they prepare it together? In the post-game interview, Karjakin said no. Mamedyarov actually admitted that he had been involved

Magnus Carlsen's suggestion that Shakhriyar Mamedyarov's draw against Sergey Karjakin had been prearranged, was denied by the players, but nevertheless led to a heated discussion.

0-0 9.♘c3 People really do a lot to avoid the Marshall these days, but the line with the knight to c3 is not easy to understand for a classical player. **9...♘a5 10.♗a2 ♗e6 11.b4 ♗xa2 12.♖xa2 ♘c6**

This has been played a few times at the highest level, and not all games ended in a draw. However, MVL was just happy to put an end to a relatively weak tournament, while Magnus said it was risky to avoid the repetition. **13.♗g5 ♘g4 14.♗d2 ♘f6 15.♗g5 ♘g4 16.♗d2 ♘f6 17.♗g5** Draw.

There seemed to be no good reason for a pre-arranged draw here, and it obviously wasn't, but it gave us something else to think about. This is not the Magnus we're used to. Is it a sign of lessened ambitions? To everyone's surprise, he just seemed to be happy with a short day at work. He even seemed satisfied with his shared second place in the tournament. I hope this will not be the case in London in November. ■

in pre-arranged draws before – many players undoubtedly have! – but not this time. The rules are simple. Both players must be given a 0 if a draw was prearranged, but this hardly ever happens, both because it's hard to prove and (perhaps) because it's so widespread and common. Perhaps it's time to do something about it. The best players in the world have a special responsibility, of course, but both Karjakin and Mamedyarov are respected fighters, so the discussion should not be connected with them and this game.

As someone joked, referring to Magnus' suggestion about the Mamedyarov-Karjakin game, his own last-round game against Maxime Vachier-Lagrave could also easily be taken for a pre-arranged draw. After all, MVL was one of Magnus' seconds before the last World Championship match, and they had looked at precisely this line together, as Magnus explained in the 'confession booth', the invention by the Norwegian broadcast channel TV2 in which the players divulge their thoughts during the game.

Maxime Vachier-Lagrave
Magnus Carlsen
Norway Chess 2018 (9)
Ruy Lopez

1.e4 e5
When questioned about the quick outcome, Magnus said that he perhaps should have chosen something else on move 1. 'I was very unsure of what to do. Basically I just decided in the car on the way here to play my normal stuff and see what happened. And as you could see, nothing happened.'
2.♘f3 ♘c6 3.♗b5 a6 4.♗a4 ♘f6 5.0-0 ♗e7 6.d3 b5 7.♗b3 d6 8.a3

Stavanger 2018												cat. XXII	
				1	2	3	4	5	6	7	8	9	TPR
1 Fabiano Caruana	IGM	USA	2822	*	0	½	1	1	1	½	½	½	1	5	2871
2 Magnus Carlsen	IGM	NOR	2843	1	*	½	½	0	1	½	½	½	4½	2824
3 Hikaru Nakamura	IGM	USA	2769	½	½	*	½	½	½	½	½	1	4½	2833
4 Vishy Anand	IGM	IND	2760	0	½	½	*	½	½	½	1	1	4½	2834
5 Wesley So	IGM	USA	2778	0	1	½	½	*	½	½	½	½	4	2792
6 Levon Aronian	IGM	ARM	2764	½	0	½	½	½	*	1	½	½	4	2794
7 Shakhriyar Mamedyarov	IGM	AZE	2808	½	½	½	½	½	0	*	½	½	3½	2748
8 Maxime Vachier-Lagrave	IGM	FRA	2789	½	½	½	0	½	½	½	*	0	3	2707
9 Sergey Karjakin	IGM	RUS	2782	0	½	0	0	½	½	½	1	*	3	2708

Ding Liren had to withdraw after 3 rounds – his results, 3 draws, were not counted

YE RONGGUANG

Adorned with a crown of flowers, a beaming Ju Wenjun gives her winner's speech. Looking for new challenges the 6th Chinese Women's World Champion would love to play a match against Hou Yifan. And, just like Hou Yifan, play more in men's tournaments.

A perfect day
for 'little jellyfish'

**Ju Wenjun
Women's World
Champion**

In an all-Chinese final, Ju Wenjun defeated reigning champion Tan Zhongyi 5½-4½ to become FIDE's new Women's World Champion. Our reporter **JILIN ZHANG** closely followed the match and talked to the winner. We also bring you two key games annotated by the new champ.

Now that Hou Yifan – rated 2658 and easily the world's best female player – no longer takes part in the Women's World Championship, the title has evidently lost some of its glamour. Nevertheless, interest in China in the match between Tan Zhongyi and her challenger, the winner of the 2015/16 Women's Grand Prix, Ju Wenjun, was considerable. After Ju Wenjun had claimed the match and the 120,000 euros that came with the title, there was impressive attention from the media, and she even appeared on the national evening news, a privilege normally reserved for Olympic champions.

One reason for the widespread public interest must have been that it was clear that China would have another World Champion (the 6th in the women's competition). Another explanation was that the match promised to be very close. Perhaps Ju Wenjun (2571) was slightly favourite, but Tan Zhongyi (2522) is known to be a tenacious fighter.

Both players were born in 1991 (when Xie Jun became the first Chinese World Champion), spent many years growing up together in the national team, and ended up going to the same university. In fact, it was Tan Zhongyi who first came up with Ju Wenjun's nickname, which, roughly translated, is 'Little Jellyfish'. For readers who regularly compete in pub quizzes: The nickname originated when Ju Wenjun and her friends used to play a computer game in which Ju Wenjun was in charge of killing the jellyfish.

Before the match, there were lively discussions on Chinese social media, and even their colleagues agreed that 'anything could happen'. Looking back, Ju Wenjun said: 'I felt a lot of pressure. After all I had to challenge someone. I wasn't sure about anything and sometimes I had trouble sleeping. Now I am much more relaxed, and

during the match I learned that I should just try my best and forget about the result.'

Two cities

The match was divided into two parts. The first five games were played in Ju Wenjun's home city of Shanghai, the second half in Tan Zhongyi's place of birth, Chongqing, a huge city some one thousand miles west of Shanghai. Ju Wenjun enjoyed the support of her family. 'My mum visited me every day when we were playing in Shanghai and she kept me company in Chongqing. She was very nervous and couldn't go to sleep because she worried so much about my games. But when I won, she

'Ju is my family name, Wenjun means my parents wish me to become a well-educated person with a noble character.'

was the most excited of us all. My dad was also happy, but he managed to keep his composure.'

The match was essentially decided in Shanghai, where Jun Wenjun took a two-point lead thanks to three wins and only one loss. Arriving in Chongqing, she also lost Game 6 after a long fight of 125 moves, but in the remaining games she defended her lead without any great problems.

She attributed much of her success to her team, which included GMs Wang Yue and Ni Hua. With Ni Hua, who also lives in Shanghai, she trained intensely for the past year. With great fondness and respect she calls him 'teacher'. 'During the match I realized that being a trainer is not easy. In Game 8, I had an easy win, but I missed it and eventually it was a draw. It was like missing a match point. When I saw him, he looked so tired and disappointed, but he still needed to comfort me and say it didn't matter.'

The hard-working type

Ju Wenjun was born in Shanghai. As for all Chinese people, her name carries the best wishes from her parents: 'Ju is my family name, Wenjun means my parents wish me to become a well-educated person with a noble character.' She started playing chess at the age of seven. Seeing her interest, her father tried several schools for her, hoping to find an ideal environment for her to learn chess. Compared to the young chess stars, she wasn't outstanding in her earlier years, but her interest in chess kept her going.

She considers herself the hard-working type and she has been serious and independent from a young age. In primary school, she started going to her chess lessons by herself, taking the bus. 'My parents were very busy with their work, and I felt I could travel between home, school and chess classes by myself.' In high school, Ju Wenjun used her pocket money to buy her mum a birthday cake. 'It was so big that it took us days to finish. That was the point when my mum realized I'd grown up'.

Chess always remained a fun activity for her. 'I don't seem to have many childhood memories except for playing chess. Even when I was sick, I wouldn't miss my chess lessons. It was all pure interest. I think playing chess provides a good opportunity to travel to different places and communicate with people from different cultures. One special memory I have was that one time I went to Qingdao to play a national youth event. I spent some time at the beach playing with seaweed. Somehow that image comes back to me even today. I was very, very happy.'

Werewolf Kill

Her progress was never explosive; it was more a gradual natural development. Around 2003 it happened that the Shanghai team needed some new blood, and from all the promising young girls they picked her. She wasn't ready to become a professional chess player just yet, but she thought it was a good opportunity and wanted to give it a try. After her recruitment into the Shanghai team everything went smoothly for her, and in 2004 she was given the chance to train in the National Team in Beijing, where she would spend the next years. 'I remember clearly when, in 2008, Coach Li Wenliang notified me that I would play in the Olympiad. That was one of the most exciting moments in my life. I remember I ran all the way from the third floor, where we were training, through the courtyard and all the way to the street. I was so excited. I just couldn't stop running!'

Three years ago she moved back to Shanghai, where she is currently living with her parents. She continues to spend a lot of time on training, sometimes more than six hours a day. Besides chess, she likes going for a walk in the park, running or doing other physical exercise. 'It is important to maintain physical strength. One needs lots of energy to play tough chess games.' And she likes to watch videos. 'I am mainly into mind game videos. Like, I've been following a card game called "Werewolf Kill", where you watch other people playing the game online and listen to their live commentating.'

When I ask her if she has a boyfriend, she is reluctant and says she prefers not to speak about it. As I can see that she is serious, I ask her about further pastimes and interests. She admits that she likes fashion. High heels, polished nails, she loves it. 'I quite enjoy shopping, looking for nice dresses or accessories.'

And she is very interested in history. 'I like to watch "The Lecture Room", a historical program with great stories about the old dynasties. There have been so many excellent people that achieved extraordinary

things in the past from which we can still learn today.'

Talking about modern people that inspire her, she mentions the musician Jay Chou. 'During the match, Jay Chou released a new piece with very cool lyrics and I just kept listening to it.'

Challenges ahead

As for the near future, her ambitions are obviously connected to chess. Winning the World Championship title is not going to be the end of her career. 'I still want to focus on chess for at least two years and see how far I can go.' Some fans in China would love to see her play a match with Hou Yifan. 'If the opportunity arises, I'd love to play. I think one should always look for challenges to improve.'

Some people say it is a bit unfortunate for her to have been born in the same era as Hou Yifan, but Ju Wenjun disagrees. 'Hou Yifan is a very talented and hardworking chess player. She deserves her success. Her achievements are an inspiration for me.'

And, just like Hou Yifan, she'd like to play more in men's tournaments. If it was up to her, she'd like to play China's number one, Ding Liren. 'But I will have to increase my rating first, at least to 2630.'

The opening moves of Game 1. The first half of the match was played in Ju Wenjun's home city of Shanghai, the second half in Tan Zhongyi's place of birth, Chongqing.

NOTES BY
Ju Wenjun

Ju Wenjun
Tan Zhongyi
Shanghai 2018 (3)
Catalan Opening

I had won the second game and was leading 1½-½. I was playing White, so I was ready to fight and play for a win again.

1.d4 d5 2.c4 e6 This time, my opponent refuses the Queen's Gambit, but I was not surprised. Playing different lines is part of her style, and this time, too, I was wondering what she would play.

3.♘f3 ♘f6 4.g3

I had done some preparation in the Catalan before the match.

4...dxc4 5.♗g2 ♘c6

This is a common variation against the Catalan. Now White has many lines to choose from; 6.♕a4 is solid for White,

but maybe not too dangerous for Black. So I went for something else.
6.0-0!? ♖b8 7.♘c3
This move will lead to chaos.

7...b5 Another interesting line was 7...a6 8.e4 ♗e7 9.♕e2 b5 10.♖d1 0-0 11.d5 exd5 12.e5 d4 13.exf6 ♗xf6, with compensation for the piece for Black.
8.♘e5 ♘xe5 9.dxe5 ♘d7 10.♕c2
Actually, I had played the same line against Tan in 2013, a game that she won. Now she tried to find out if there was a hidden trick in the position and started playing slowly. It somewhat surprised me that she did not seem well-prepared for this line.
10...♗b7 11.♗xb7 ♖xb7 12.♖d1

12...♗e7? Played after a long think. More common is 12...♕c8, which is what she played in our game that I just mentioned, in Wuxi in 2013.
13.♕e4!? I realized that 12...♗e7 must be a bad move, since ♕e4, followed by ♕g4, is a very logical continuation for White now, stopping Black from castling kingside in view of ♗h6!.
13...♕c8 14.♕g4?!
But stronger was 14.a4 c6 (14...b4 15.♘b5) 15.♕g4! g6 16.♗h6 ♘xe5

17.♕h3 ♖g8 18.♗f4 ♘d7 19.♘e4!, and White is better.

14...g5?? Played after thinking for about 20 minutes. I was shocked, because any move is better than ...g5. 14...g6, for instance, is pretty good, and I still have no idea how to react to that move. Other options were 14...♔f8 or 14...♗f8. Maybe she felt some pressure. That would be a logical reason why she made such a blunder. This may also serve as good advice for young players: do not push ...g5 or ...g4 in the early opening (unless you are Richard Rapport).
After 14...g6! the play might continue 15.♗h6 ♘xe5 16.♕h3 (16.♕f4 f6 17.♘e4 ♔f7 is unclear) 16...♖g8 17.♗f4 ♘d7 (♘e4 is not a threat now) 18.♕xh7 ♘f6, and Black is fine.
15.♕h5! Here I felt that I was going to win. Black's position is really bad.

15...♘c5 After 15...♘xe5 16.♗xg5 White is winning.
Maybe 15...♕d8 was the best defence, but Black's pieces are rather passive, and her king is left in the middle. After 16.♘e4 h6 17.f4 White is better.
16.♗xg5 c6 17.♖d4 Here, 17.♗f6 was an easy win, which I missed. But OK, the text-move is not bad either.

Ju Wenjun

Born: January 31, 1991, Shanghai, China

Career highlights
2008: Chinese League Champion
2009: Gold with China at Women's World Teams
2009: Chinese League Champion
2010: Chinese Women's Champion
2010: Gold with China at Asian Teams
2011: Gold with China at World Teams
2012: Chinese League Champion
2014: Chinese Women's Champion
2014: FIDE Grand Prix, Sharjah, 1st
2016: FIDE Grand Prix, Tehran, 1st
2016: FIDE Grand Prix, Khanty-Mansiysk, 1st
2016: Overall winner 2015/16 FIDE Grand Prix
2016: Gold with China at Baku Olympiad
2016: Chinese League Champion
2017: Gibraltar Chess Festival Top Female
2017: Chinese League Champion
2017: Riyadh, Women's World Rapid Champion
2018: Women's World Champion

17...♘d7 18.♗xe7 ♔xe7 19.♕h4+ ♔e8 20.♖ad1

20...♕d8? After 20...♖xd4 21.♕xd4 ♘d7 22.♘e4 White also wins.
21.♕f4? This is a serious inaccuracy. After 21.♕xd8+ ♔xd8 22.♘e4! White wins on the spot.

21...♖xd4 22.♖xd4 ♕b6 23.♖d6

Still, Black continues to suffer. White will trade off the knights and attack the c6-pawn.

23...♖f8 24.♘e4 ♘xe4 25.♕xe4 ♕b7 26.♖xc6 ♔d7 27.♕d4+

Black resigned, since 27...♔xc6 allows 28.♕d6 mate. This was a quick game, which lasted about three hours. I was on plus-2 and felt confident.

**NOTES BY
Ju Wenjun**

**Tan Zhongyi
Ju Wenjun**
Shanghai 2018 (5)
Bishop's Opening

I had lost the fourth game and had a free day before this round, Game 5. A funny story is what happened at the start of the second half of the match when I arrived at the hotel, which was located in the city centre of Chongqing. Because I was staying on the 21st floor, I asked if my room would give me a view of the Huangpu river. The answer was no, you cannot see the

Huangpu river. And at my puzzled look: But there's the Suzhou river! On our free day, my coach and I went out and walked across a bridge with the Suzhou river flowing beneath. But back to the game! I was still leading by one point. My opponent's play in her previous games has given me no indication of how and what I should prepare, so I just took it easy.

1.e4!? A new challenge. She had never played 1.e4 before. She had evidently prepared something, so I tried to play solidly.

1...e5 2.♗c4 Avoiding the Petroff. Naiditsch had played 2.♗c4 against me in last year's Isle of Man tournament, a game that I lost. Maybe she had prepared something based on that game.

2...♘f6 3.d3

3...c6 She seemed a bit surprised by this move. On a previous occasion I had gone 3...♗c5.

4.♘f3 d5 5.♗b3 a5 6.a4 ♗b4+ 7.c3 ♗d6

8.0-0!? More popular is 8.exd5 cxd5 9.♗g5 ♗e6 10.♘a3 ♘bd7 11.♘b5 ♗b8 12.0-0 0-0 13.♖e1, with unclear play.

8...0-0 8...dxe4 9.dxe4 0-0 10.♘bd2 ♕e7 11.♘c4 ♗c7 is interesting, but during the game I felt that ...dxe4 would only make sense if White played ♗g5; otherwise I would just waste a few tempi.

9.exd5 cxd5 10.♘a3

After 10.♗g5 ♗e6 11.♘a3 ♘bd7 it is hard to assess the position.

10...♘bd7 Better was 10...h6!? 11.♘b5 ♘c6 12.♘xd6 ♕xd6, but I preferred to keep the bishop pair.

11.♖e1?! And instead of the text-move, 11.♗g5 h6 12.♗h4 ♗b8 13.♖e1 ♖e8 was better.

11...h6! A simple and good move, stopping the idea of ♗g5 and making it difficult for White to find a move. Meanwhile, I felt that after this move, Tan would not like her position.

Shanghai/Chongqing 2018			1	2	4	5	6	7	7	8	9	10		TPR
1 Ju Wenjun	IGM CHN	2571	½	1	1	0	1	0	½	½	½	½	5½	2555
2 Tan Zhongyi	IGM CHN	2522	½	0	0	1	0	1	½	½	½	½	4½	2538

12.♘b5 ♗b8 13.d4

White wants to break Black's centre.

13...e4 14.♘d2 ♘b6 15.f3

Worse was 15.c4? ♗g4 16.♕c2 ♗f5.

15...♖e8

15...exf3? 16.♘xf3 ♗g4 17.♕d3 is clearly better for White.

16.♗c2 ♗d7

Maybe 16...♗f5 was also good, but I didn't like the position after 17.b3 ♗g6 18.♘f1, when Black is better but White's position is still playable.

17.♖b1

White loses after 17.b3? ♗xb5 18.axb5 ♕c7! 19.♘f1 ♕xc3. And after 17.fxe4 ♗g4, Black is better. 17.♖e2 is the computer's first option, but this is not a logical human move (the idea being 17...exf3 18.♘xf3 ♘e4 – 18...♘c4 – 19.♕e1!). After 17...♘c8!?, with the idea of ...♖a6 and ...♖ae6, however, Black is still better.

17...exf3 18.♘xf3 ♘e4

Here Black is slightly better.

19.♘e5!?

I was a bit surprised that she sacri-

ficed a pawn. After 19.♖f1 ♗g4 20.♕d3 ♘d7 Black's position is slightly preferable.

19...♗xe5 20.dxe5 ♗xb5 21.axb5 ♖xe5 22.♗e3 ♖e6

23.♗d4

Black would be better after 23.♗xe4 dxe4 24.♕xd8+ ♖xd8 25.♗xb6 ♖xb6 26.c4 f5 27.♖ed1 ♖xd1+ 28.♖xd1 ♔f7 29.♖d7+ ♔f6 30.♔f2 f4.

Or after 23.♕g4 ♘c4 24.♗d4 ♖g6 25.♕h3 ♕g5.

23...♘c4

All Black's pieces are directed to the kingside to launch the attack.

28.♗c2 ♘h4 29.♕d3 ♘g6

Or 29...f5!, with the idea of ...f4 and ...f3, and Black should be winning.

30.♗e3 ♕h5 31.c4?

This loses immediately. After 31.♗d1, White could still defend.

24.♗d3 ♕g5 25.b3 ♘cd6 26.♖b2 ♖ae8 27.♖be2 ♘f5!

31...♘e5! 32.♕d4

White is also lost after 32.♕xd5 ♘c3 33.♕d2 ♘xe2+ 34.♖xe2 ♘g4.

32...♖g6!

33.♗xe4

33.♔h1 runs into 33...♘f3.

33...dxe4 34.♔f1 ♘f3 35.♕d7

Or 35.gxf3 ♕h3+ 36.♔f2 ♕xf3 mate.

35...♘xh2+ White resigned.

With a bit of luck I had won this game with Black. Now I was on plus-2 again, with only five games remaining. A great advantage, as we moved to Chongqing for the second half of the match. ∎

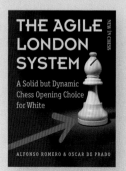

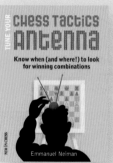

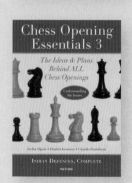

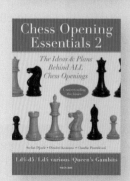

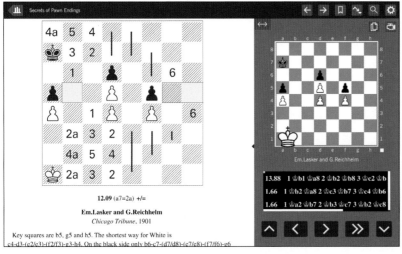
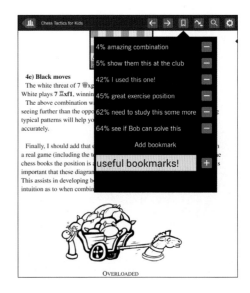

Playing against a 'god'

My missed chances against Bobby Fischer

Curaçao 1962: Pal Benko and Bobby Fischer (back row, 5th and 8th from left) together with colleagues and organizers. The two Americans stood no chance against the five Soviets (Petrosian, Keres, Geller, Kortchnoi and Tal) that decided the course of the tournament.

On July 14, **PAL BENKO** will celebrate his 90th birthday. In an interview with New In Chess at the end of 2015, he talked about the opportunities he had squandered in his games against friend and rival Bobby Fischer. On this memorable occasion, the Hungarian-American legend provides the analytical proof.

Writing about the late Walter Browne in New In Chess 2015/5, Jan Timman quoted Walter as saying, 'If Fischer is god, then I am the devil.' Timman added that Browne played only one game against 'god', in Yugoslavia in 1970. The position was clearly winning for Browne, but Fischer defended stubbornly, and after a long fight (Browne would still have had a win after the fourth time-control with 88.♖h7 instead of 88.c7?) Walter finally gave away the win.

It only looked too familiar to me. Walter was indeed my colleague, and not only in his propensity to get into time-trouble.

If you look at the games I played against Bobby Fischer, the statistics do not show a rosy picture for me. The overall score is eight wins, three losses and seven draws in Fischer's favour. I was White in eight of these 18 games. The colour division was interesting, because I lost only one game as White, the last one I could have won.

Here I would like to look at five of my games against Fischer in which I missed opportunities. Fischer was undoubtedly the best player of his time. Besides being very talented, he was well-prepared in the openings. I have to admit that I did not study openings much. I was of the opinion that you should try to find the best plans and the best moves while playing. This took more time, of course, so I usually ended up in time-trouble, from which, as we will see, Bobby would benefit.

It was especially hard to play against his 1.e4, because it was difficult to avoid forced variations. So I tried out as many as five different defences that I knew only by their general principles. It was hard to fight off his pressure, and if I managed to, I was invariably short on time.

Let's have a look at the proof of my claims. The following examples have been selected from an eight-year period when we frequently played one another at national or international level. There was always something important at stake. Recalling these games, I feel sorry for the missed chances, mainly from an artistic point of view.

Book Draw

Bobby Fischer
Pal Benko
New York US Championship 1959

position after 50...g3

The game had been adjourned after move 40 and I was there in time the next afternoon to continue. Some minutes before the clock would be started, Fischer's mother Regina phoned the arbiter saying that her son was not feeling well and that the resumption should be postponed. Hans Kmoch, the arbiter, answered that he couldn't postpone the game without a doctor's certificate, but he gave Fischer one hour to appear. This was also against the rules, of course.

I was kept waiting and had got nervous and impatient by the time the game was resumed. On top of everything, it was clear that Fischer was as fit as a fiddle, and that he had wanted to gain time for analysing the position. Despite being upset,

> ## 'It was hard to fight off Fischer's pressure, and if I managed to, I was invariably short on time.'

I managed to hold the position till move 56 when, with my flag about to fall, I blundered and presented my opponent with the full point.
51.♖d6+ ♔f7
Here 51....♔f5! also drew by supporting the passed pawn with the king.
52.♖d7+ ♔f6 53.♖d1 g2 54.♖g1 ♖g6 55.a5 ♔e7 56.a6

56...♖b6+??
A typical mistake before the second time-control: a quick check to make the control. A book draw is 56...♖xa6 57.♖xg2 ♖b6+ 58.♔a4 ♔d7 etc. The simplest one amongst various alternatives.
57.♔a5 ♖xb3 58.♖xg2 ♖a3+ 59.♔b6 ♖b3+ 60.♔c5 ♖a3 61.a7 ♔e6 62.♖g7 ♖a1 63.♔c6

♖a2 64.♔b7 ♖b2+ 65.♔c8 ♖a2 66.♔b8 ♖b2+ 67.♖b7 ♖h2 68.a8♕ ♖h8+ 69.♔a7
Black resigned.

One Mistake

Pal Benko
Bobby Fischer
Belgrade Candidates 1959
Sicilian Defence, Najdorf Variation
1.e4 c5 2.♘f3 d6 3.d4 cxd4 4.♘xd4 ♘f6 5.♘c3 a6 6.♗c4 ♘bd7 7.a4! g6 8.0-0 ♗g7 9.♗g5 0-0 10.♕d2 ♘c5 11.f3 ♗d7 12.a5 ♖c8 13.b3 ♘e6 14.♗e3 ♕c7 15.♘de2 ♗c6 16.♖a2 ♘d7 17.♘d5 ♕d8 18.♘ec3 ♘c7 19.♘b4 ♘e5 20.♗e2 ♕e8 21.♘a4 ♗xa4 22.♖xa4 ♘c6 23.♘d5 ♘xd5 24.exd5 ♘e5 25.♗d4 ♕d8 26.f4 ♘d7 27.♗xg7 ♔xg7 28.♗g4 ♖c5 29.♗xd7 ♕xd7 30.f5 f6 31.fxg6 hxg6 32.♖h4 g5 33.♖e4 ♕c7 34.c4 ♖xa5 35.h4 gxh4

Confronting Fischer with his own opening weapon against the Najdorf (6.♗c4), I had forced him onto unusual territory and had manoeuvred effectively to gain a significant space advantage. I could have been proud of this, if only I had finished the job. White is winning, but I had not much time left for the rest.
36.♖fe1!?
The best was 36.♕e2! e5 37.♕h5, or 36....♖f7 37.♖xh4, and this should have been winning. The simple 36.♖xh4 was slower, but also good.
36...e5

37.dxe6?? This lets the locked-out rook back into the game to join the defence. Instead, 37.♖xh4 ♖g8 38.♕h6+ ♔f7 39.♕h7+ ♔g7 40.♕f5 ♕e7 41.♖h8 would still have been hopeless for Black.

37...♖g5 38.♖xh4 ♕c5+ 39.♕f2 Still better for White was 39.♖e3, but I tried to play it safe.

39....♖e5 40.♕xc5 ♖xe1+ 41.♔f2 dxc5 42.♔xe1 And by now Black was somewhat better, but it was a draw after 64 moves.

Forgetfulness

Bobby Fischer
Pal Benko
Curaçao Candidates 1962 (8)

position after 19.♘xe6

It is hard to explain why I now immediately played **19...♗xe6??** considering that I had planned 19...♗xb2+ 20.♔xb2 ♕b4+ 21.♔c1 ♕a3+ 22.♔d2 ♕a5+, which would have forced an immediate draw. After this missed opportunity I may have had other drawing lines, but I completely failed to get over this mistake. When I resigned, I told Fischer that I could

have forced a draw. 'You never had a draw', answered Bobby. When I showed him 19...♗xb2+ 20.♔xb2 ♕b4+ 21.♔c1 ♕a3+ 22.♔d2 ♕a5+, he was surprised.

20.♕xe6+ ♔h8 21.♔b1 ♕xf2 22.♕xf5 ♕xf5 23.♗xf5 g6 24.♗d3 ♖ad8 25.h5

25...♔g7 26.hxg6 hxg6 27.♗xb5 ♖xd1+ 28.♖xd1 ♖b8 29.a4 a6 30.♖d7+ ♔h6 31.♖d6 ♗xb2 32.♔xb2 axb5 33.a5 ♖a8 34.a6 ♔h5 35.♔b3 g5 36.♔b4 ♔g4 37.♔xb5 ♔g3 38.♖d7 g4 39.a7 Black resigned.

Bobby once told me: 'If I see a pawn hanging without reason, I take it.' Anyhow, after the game I analysed the diagrammed position with Tal, the attacker, and Petrosian, the defender. I was in the middle.

position after 18...♗f6

Instead of **19.♘xe6**, we looked at the more interesting 19.♕h5, and now 19...h6 20.♕g6 hxg5 21.hxg5 ♗e5 22.♖h7 ♖f7 23.♗c4! bxc4 24.♖d8+ ♕f8 25.♕h5 g6 26.♕xg6+ ♗g7

27.♖d1!! (Tal) 27...♕c5 28.♖dh1 ♔f8 29.♖xg7! ♖xg7 30.♖h8+ ♔e7 31.♕xg7+ ♔d6 32.♕f8+ ♔d5 33.♕xc5+ ♔xc5 34.g6, and White wins.

This is all nice but not forced. Instead of 21...♗e5, things are not so clear after 21....♗xb2+ 22.♔xb2 ♕b4+, although it seems that White has a serious initiative.

Many Winning Lines

Bobby Fischer
Pal Benko
Curaçao Candidates 1962 (22)
French Defence, Steinitz Variation
1.e4 e6 2.d4 d5 3.♘c3 ♘f6 4.e5 ♘fd7 5.f4 c5 6.dxc5 ♗xc5 7.♕g4 0-0 8.♗d3 f5 9.♕h3 ♗xg1 10.♖xg1 ♘c5 11.♗d2 ♘c6 12.♘b5 ♕b6 13.0-0-0 ♗d7 14.♘d6

14....♘a4! 15.♗b5 If 15.b3, then 15...♕d4. **15...♘d4! 16.♗e3 ♘e2+ 17.♗xe2 ♕xb2+ 18.♔d2 ♕b4+ 19.♔c1 ♘c3 20.♖de1 ♘xa2+ 21.♔d1 ♘c3+ 22.♔c1 d4 23.♗f2 ♖fc8** Better was 23...♖ac8!. **24.♗d3** A mistake would be 24.♘xc8? ♕a3+ 25.♔d2 ♘e4+. **24...♘a2+ 25.♔d1**

Budapest, 1993. Although they had their conflicts, Pal Benko and Bobby Fischer always remained on good terms.

Bobby was surprised when I gave away the valuable bishop for the undeveloped g1-knight. In addition, after the early 12.♘b5 Black could attack and came up with an intuitive piece sacrifice with 15....♘d4. It looks as if Fischer thought it was only good enough for a draw; the knight on d6 is worth something, after all. But I soon made it clear that I wanted more than perpetual check. Even so, I should have repeated some more checks to gain time.

25...♘c3+ 26.♔c1 ♖c5

26...♗a4 would also have won, but was more complicated.

27.♕h4 ♖a5

This is logical, but 27...♗a4 was again very strong. The key to open the position is the c2-pawn: 28.♕e7 ♕b1+ 29.♔d2 ♘e4+ 30.♖xe4 ♖xc2+, winning, or 28.♔d2 ♖xc2! 29.♗xc2 ♘d5+ 30.♔e2 ♖xc2+ 31.♔f1 ♕d2 32.♖h1 ♘e3+ 33.♔g1 ♕xe1+ 34.♗xe1 ♖xg2 mate.

28.♔d2

An incredible move, and I have to give credit to Bobby that this is definitely the best defence against the 28...♘e4 mating threat.

28...h6?? Time-trouble. Instead, I had three winning alternatives. After the quiet 28....♗c6, White runs out of good moves, since 29.g4 ♗f3 mates. If 29.♘c4 then 29...♖a2 30.♗xd4 ♘d5+ 31.♔e2 ♖xc2+ 32.♗xc2 ♕xc4+ wins. 28...♖a2 29.g4 ♗c6 30.gxf5 ♘b1+ 31.♔e2 (or 31.♔c1 ♕a3+ 32.♔d1 ♕xd3+ 33.cxd3 ♘c3+ 34.♔c1 ♗a4, winning) 31....♕d2+ 32.♔f1 ♕xd3+ 33.cxd3 ♘d2+ 34.♔e2 ♗f3 mates nicely. And, finally, 28....♖a3, etc., also wins.

29.g4 fxg4?

At least 29.....♘d5+ should have been played, but White is already better, and a helpmate is coming.

30.♖xg4 ♔h8 31.♕xh6+

Black resigned.

No further comment on my part. The late GM Larry Evans once wrote in *Chess Life* that Benko sometimes showed suicidal tendencies at the board.

And finally, let's take a look at another annoying missed winning line against Fischer. This was the only game I lost against him with the white pieces.

Doubly Short-sighted

Pal Benko
Robert Fischer
New York US Championship 1966

position after 23...♗h6

24.♖e1 It is heart-breaking that I lost this position, since I needed to calculate only one move deeper to find the winning continuation: 24.♘xe8 (or 24.♘xa8) 24...♗xc1 25.♘c7 ♗xb2 26.♖b1 ♖c8 27.♘d5 ♖c2

ANALYSIS DIAGRAM

This looked so strong that I did not look any further, but now 28.♘e3 would have decided the game in my favour. Unfortunately, I saw it too late. The next day Fischer cele-

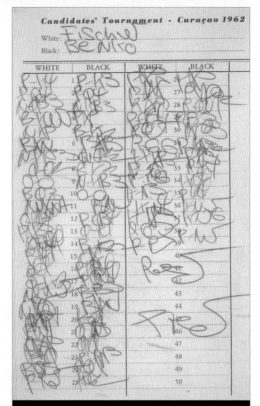

Bobby Fischer's scoresheet of his game against Pal Benko in Round 8 of the Curaçao Candidates.

brated his great game. When I showed him how he could have lost, he was speechless. He had also been looking at the line up to 27...♖c2, and had also missed that 28.♘e3! wins. The game continued:

24...♖ec8 25.♘xa8 ♖c2 26.♖xe2?
This was not necessary, since 26.♔g1 ♗f3 27.♗h3 ♘e2+ 28.♔f2 ♘d4+ 29.♔g1 was a draw.

26...♖xe2+ 27.♔f1 ♖xb2 28.♗c3 ♖c2 29.♗xd4 exd4 30.e5 ♗e3

31.♗xb7? The decisive error. After 31.♗e4 or 31.♖e1 the game is still unclear, although Black has the initiative

31...♖f2+ 32.♔e1 d3 33.♗a6 ♖e2+ 34.♔d1 ♖xh2 35.♗xd3 ♖d2+ 36.♔e1 ♖xd3 37.♔e2 ♖a3 38.♘c7 ♗d4 39.♘b5

39...♗xa1 40.♘xa3 ♗xe5 41.g4 ♔g7 42.♘c4 ♔f6 White resigned.

We can see from all these examples that even Fischer did not see everything. He also made mistakes, albeit not very often. In any case, he never got into time-trouble. So we should not call him a chess god, only a demi-god.

In a recent enjoyable article in *Chess Life* about his own return to chess, GM Jim Tarjan wrote that chess in America might have been better off without Fischer. A strange statement, for which he did not provide an explanation.

I think nobody has achieved more for American chess than Fischer. His match for the World Championship in 1972 in Reykjavik was followed by everyone in the US and created worldwide interest. Even people who had never heard about the game before were following the match. Membership of the USCF doubled. Prizes at tournaments became more decent and some players could make a modest living by teaching chess.

Unfortunately, we have to separate Fischer's human side from his chess career. He definitely had mental problems, which he never admitted to and never looked for help for. This contributed to his early death. Just like Paul Morphy, he became the 'pride and sorrow' of American Chess. ∎

ENDGAME TURBO 5
ON USB STICK

Get the Endgame Turbo 5 and turn your chess program into an endgame genius! Simply plug the stick into the computer. No need for an installation on the hard disk. Superfast access via USB 3.0!

There was never anything like that from ChessBase!

With the new Endgame Turbo 5 there is for the first time a ChessBase product on a USB stick. The new Turbo offers perfect endgame analyses and a mighty gain in performance for your engines in the endgame. Thanks to the economical data format (Syzygy) the Endgame Turbo 5 is faster and includes clearly more types of endgame than the previous versions. The volume of the endgame databases is 128 GB (on the USB stick) – that represents the contents of 27 DVDs!

For all endgame positions with 3, 4 and 5 pieces, as well as for 143 of the most important 6-piece positions the new Turbo 5 has the precise evaluation of the position for you to access immediately. So with the programs ChessBase 13/14, Fritz 15/16, Komodo 11 and Houdini 6 you can establish in no time at all whether an endgame position is won, lost or drawn and what the path to the draw or win

looks like. Over and above that, the programs Komodo Chess 11 and Houdini 6 also use the knowledge of the Endgame Turbo during their analysis of endgames with more than six pieces, e.g. whenever during their calculation of variations it is possible to evaluate liquidations into endgames with six or fewer pieces. Thus these engines more quickly reach more precise and reliable results and clearly improve your playing strength.

Using Endgame Turbo 5 is childishly easy: plugging the USB stick into the computer automatically starts an initialisation which only takes one or two seconds. Done and dusted! From then on your Fritz or ChessBase program is, in combination with the Endgame Turbo 5 USB stick, a real endgame genius! There is no need to install the endgame databases on the hard disk.

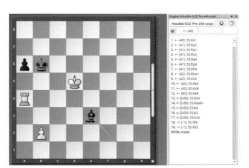

Endgame expert Dr. Karsten Müller:
"Previously the analyses of complicated endgames were often mysterious. The rise of the computer shone light into many dark corners. But not till Tablebases could all the beauty and incredible depth of the royal game be shown to full advantage. The new Endgame Turbo 5 is indispensable for the decryption of complex endgames and also for my own analyses!"

ENDGAME TURBO 5 ON USB STICK 179,90 €

ChessBase GmbH · News: en.chessbase.com · CB Shop: shop.chessbase.com
CHESSBASE DEALER: NEW IN CHESS · P.O. Box 1093 · NL-1810 KB Alkmaar
phone (+31)72 5127137 · fax (+31)72 5158234 · WWW.NEWINCHESS.COM

Play It Again, Sam...

US Champion follows up with wins in Havana and Montevideo

There seems to be no stopping the surging Sam Shankland after his surprise capture of the US Championship crown. The California GM showed that his St. Louis title win was no fluke with a further brace of tournament

Sam Shankland received a hero's welcome during his lecture at the Mechanics' Chess Club in San Francisco, here showing his final round win in Havana over Cuban GM Yusnel Bacallao.

victories at the Capablanca Memorial in Havana and the American Continental Championship in Montevideo. **JOHN HENDERSON** looks at the remarkable recent run of the new American chess hero.

Back in late April, Sam Shankland's US Championship win in St. Louis was being hailed by many as one of the most amazing individual performances in the long and storied history of the venerable national title. After all, he defied all the pre-tournament odds with a remarkable victory ahead of three of the world's top 10 players – and he did it with more than just a touch of élan, by dramatically out-pacing the very much in-form World Championship Challenger, Fabiano Caruana, going down the home stretch.

But after the dust had finally settled in St. Louis, and the champion had collected his $50,000 winner's cheque from Rex Sinquefield, a good part of the online chatter was about how this was a one-off fluke, a not-to-be-repeated victory. The naysayers were adamant that Shankland would never be able to repeat his success, as he 'couldn't play like that again.' But they were quickly proved wrong, and how, as Sam did indeed play like that again... and again!

Just a week after his big rating spike in St. Louis and crashing through the 2700-barrier, Sam was back in action, only this time the newly-minted US champion was himself the top-seed and heading the six-player, double round-robin field at the 53rd Capablanca Memorial in Havana, Cuba. Still on a roll, he didn't disappoint his new fans by again obliterating the opposition with yet another storming performance for a second, mind-blowing 2800+ result. He won the title with an unbeaten score of 7/10, to finish a full 1½ points clear of his nearest rival, Alexey Dreev of Russia. Along the way he also created a little history by becoming the first American winner of the tournament. Shankland's favourite game from Havana was the demolition of Russian Aleksandr Rakhmanov that came midway through a three-game winning streak. That streak moved him into the sole lead, after which there was no looking back.

NOTES BY
Sam Shankland

Sam Shankland
Aleksandr Rakhmanov
Havana 2018 (6)
English Opening

After my win at the US Championship there was no rest for the wicked, as I had to travel to Havana for the Capablanca Memorial just a week later. It's a common phenomenon that you play badly right after a huge

'The naysayers were adamant that Shankland would never be able to repeat his success.'

success, and one that I experienced myself after the 2014 Olympiad in Baku [where he won the gold medal on the Reserve board with a score of 9/10 and a 2831 performance, and then had a poor start and withdrew from an Open in Riga – ed.], but I was very glad to have avoided this pitfall the second time around and score another very good result. My favourite game was this effort against Aleksandr Rakhmanov.

1.c4 e6 2.g3 d5 3.♗g2 g6

This system is a little unorthodox, but also not easy to prove an edge against. Still, I had noticed my opponent had played it a couple times before, so I had come prepared.

4.♘f3 ♗g7 5.d4 ♘c6?! I think this is inaccurate. I would prefer to develop with 5...♘e7 6.0-0 0-0, since now Black can remain flexible with the b8-knight. In some cases it may wish to go to d7, for example after 7.♘c3, I believe Black should play 7...♘d7!, when the threat of ...dxc4 is actually quite annoying. With the knight on c6, White would always have a move like ♕a4 to get the pawn back. Here this is not the case.

6.0-0 ♘ge7 7.e3 0-0

Now we see why the knight on c6 is a little misplaced. White can comfortably bring his own queen's knight out to its best square on c3 without fearing for the safety of his c4-pawn.

8.♘c3! b6 After 8...dxc4 9.♕a4, White is a bit better, thanks in no small part to the knight being on c6. If it had been on d7, ...♘d7-b6 would have been be an important resource for Black.

9.♕e2 ♗a6 10.b3 dxc4
Everything up to here was preparation, but now I was on my own. I realized I should not try to take the pawn back directly, since this would allow ...♘a5 followed by ...c5, so I developed my pieces instead, leaving bxc4 as a possibility for later.

11.♗a3! Exploiting the pin. Black cannot take on b3, of course.
Taking the pawn back at once with 11.bxc4? is far too hasty. Black has good play after 11...♘a5! 12.♘b5 c6 (12...♘xc4!?) 13.♘a3 ♖c8, with ...c6-c5 to follow.

11...♖e8 Black did not have many other options. Trying to hold on to the c4-pawn would have led to dire consequences.
Of course, 11...cxb3? is impossible in view of 12.♕xa6, while 11...♘a5? loses

a piece to 12.b4!, with b5 to follow. Finally, 11...b5? 12.♘e4! leaves Black with horribly weak squares on the queenside, and he will probably still lose a pawn there.

12.♖ac1! Remaining patient and dealing with the 'threat' of ...♘d5.

12...♕d7 13.♖fd1 ♖ad8

At long last, it is time to take the pawn back. It makes sense, since White's pieces have now found all of their best squares; but I was still hoping to take with a piece on c4. Luckily, I managed to resist the temptation to play ♘f3-d2.

14.bxc4! 14.♘d2 was very tempting, trying to take on c4 with the knight and keep the c-file open. But it is incorrect. Black has several good tries here, but the one that concerned me the most was 14...e5!? 15.d5 ♘d4! 16.exd4 exd4, with obvious counterplay.

14...♕c8 The typical move here. 14...♘a5, attacking the c4-pawn to try to get ...c7-c5 in, now fails to achieve its desired result. After, for example, 15.♘e5 ♕c8 (15...♗xe5? is even worse: 16.dxe5 ♕c8 17.♘e4, winning) 16.♘b5 Black's position looks very unpleasant.

15.♘b5 ♘a5

I had several good options here, but I took a positional approach.

SUDDENLY SAM SHANKLAND IS WINNING WHEREVER HE GOES

16.♘d2 The knight is heading to b3. It was even stronger to challenge the a5-knight immediately with 16.♗b4!, considering that after something like 16...♘ec6 17.♗c3 the bishop is better placed on c3, where it can support either e3-e4 or d4-d5, while the knight on c6 is misplaced because it prevents Black from playing ...c7-c6. This was a bit more to the point than my chosen move.

16...♕d7?

I suspect this was based on a miscalculation. My opponent may have thought this move prevents ♘d2-b3. Still, even after the best move, Black is just worse. Following 16...♖b8 17.♘b3 ♘xb3 18.axb3 ♗b7 19.♘c3, White's big centre promises him a pleasant advantage with no risk. Black is facing a long and difficult defensive task.

17.♘b3! Anyway. The point is that 17...♘xc4 does not work.

17...♘xb3 A sad necessity.

17...♘xc4? was tempting but poor: 18.♗xe7! (an important resource). Black loses material, since after 18...♖xe7 19.♘xa7! he will be unable to deal with the twin threats of ♖xc4 and ♘a7-c6.

18.axb3 Black's position is absolutely miserable.

18...♘c8 19.d5! Not the only good move, but the most direct one.

19...e5 Now White definitely should not allow ...♗xb5. Black would surely have liked to get a position like the one after 19...♗xb5 20.cxb5 e5, and if he can play ...♗g7-f8-d6 he will have decent defensive chances. But White gets there first with 21.d6!, and the threat of 22.♗c6 is decisive.

20.♘c3 ♘d6 21.♕a2!
The threat of 22.♗xd6 forces Black's bishop back, which allows the pawns to start running.
21...♗c8 22.b4! c5 is coming.
22...a6 23.c5 ♘b5 24.♘xb5 ♕xb5 I was expecting 24...axb5, trying to blunt the a3-bishop, but Black's position still looks awful.
25.♕c2 e4 I was very proud of my play at this moment. My instincts told me that 26.♗xe4 should be winning somehow, but after struggling for a while I correctly passed it up in favour of a simpler move, which is much stronger.

26.♗f1! Black's queen is forced to the extremely inconvenient d7-square, where it will block in the c8-bishop and be harassed by White's advancing central pawns.
Tempting as it was to take the pawn with 26.♗xe4? White will be unable to consolidate: 26...bxc5! 27.bxc5 ♕a5!, and there is nothing to be done about the a3-bishop hanging.
Including a capture on b6 before taking e4 does not help either, since after 26.cxb6?! cxb6 27.♗xe4? Black can play 27...♗g4 28.f3 ♗xf3! 29.♗xf3 ♖xe3.
26...♕d7 27.d6!

White has a simple but completely crushing threat in c5-c6, which compels Black to make an undesirable exchange on c5.
27...bxc5
27...cxd6 is even worse, since after 28.♖xd6 the b6-pawn falls too.
28.bxc5 cxd6 29.♖xd6!
Correctly choosing the c-file for the passed pawn. It will easily get to c6, when advancing to c7 is far easier than advancing to d7 would have been. White is much better after 29.cxd6 as well, but the text is far more convincing.
29...♕c7 30.♖xd8 ♕xd8
30...♖xd8 31.♕xe4 is obviously lost for Black.
31.♕a4!

White is winning. The c-pawn is incredibly strong, and the a6-pawn should just drop. White also has a crushing threat that my opponent seems to have missed, but that only made the game shorter. The outcome would have been the same if he had played a better move.
31...h5? 32.♖d1!
Now White gains a lot of tempi. The queen is hit and must stay in touch with the e8-rook.

32...♕e7 33.c6!
Another tempo. c7 is coming next.
33...♕c7 34.♗d6 ♕b6 35.c7 ♖e6 36.♗f4

Black cannot stop ♖d8+. I had to be a little careful, but a few accurate moves finished the game very quickly.
36...g5 37.♖d8+ ♔h7 38.♖xc8 gxf4 39.♕d7!
No ghosts. Black's kingside counterplay is not so intimidating and White queens the pawn right away.
39...fxe3 40.♖b8 exf2+ 41.♔g2 ♕e3

42.♕xf7! The last accurate move, stopping 42...♕f3+. Black cannot prevent a new queen from showing up, so he resigned.

■ ■ ■

Following his win in Havana, Shankland barely had time to reflect on his two epic back-to-back performances, as he had to pack his bags again, this time heading to Montevideo in Uruguay for the American Continental Championship. And once again he was 'in the zone' with a third successive powerful performance, capturing the $5,000 first prize and the big bonus of one of the four automatic spots to the 2019 FIDE World Cup in Khanty-Mansiysk, as he finished undefeated on 9/11, a half point ahead of Argentine Grandmaster, Diego Flores.

In the space of just two months and a trifecta of tournament victories, Sam Shankland has become one of the hottest players in the world. The American has gone an awe-inspiring, Bobby Fischer-like 'My 60 Memorable Games' without a loss (in classical chess), last being beaten by French IM Anthony Bellaiche, in the penultimate round of the Biel Masters B tournament in Switzerland back in the summer of 2017. And with this unbeaten 60 games streak, Sam has seen a meteoric rise in his rating to the very prosaic 2727 and the number 27 spot on the live rating list.

Perhaps a little overawed by the enormity of his consecutive successes, Shankland was honest enough to admit that his play in Montevideo wasn't anywhere near as good as it had been in St. Louis and Havana. But when you are 'in the zone', you are 'in the zone', and the all-important clutch wins come nevertheless. His penultimate-round win over his fellow countryman, Jefferey Xiong, wasn't only important for the overall outcome of the tournament, it was, on a technical level, arguably the best game of his triple success.

NOTES BY
Sam Shankland

Jeffery Xiong
Sam Shankland
Montevideo 2018 (10)
Sicilian Defence, Najdorf Variation

Jeffery Xiong has been a tough opponent for me in the past. I have had several good positions against him, but always failed to win and even had a -1 overall score going into

this game, so I knew I had a tough challenge in front of me. I was a half point ahead of him and a draw would have been a fine result, but I decided to play a more combative line because I wanted to get a complex position.
1.e4 c5 2.♘f3 d6 3.d4 cxd4 4.♘xd4 ♘f6 5.♘c3 a6
The Najdorf was the weapon of my youth, though I don't play it much anymore. The heavy theory and many forcing lines that all seem to be worked out to a draw don't really appeal to me, but if the game leaves normal channels, I really enjoy the resulting middlegames.
6.h3

6...g6!? An unusual move, but one that I feel is undervalued. Black goes for a 'dragadorf' setup where he argues that 6.h3 is not a very useful move since White's main plan against the Dragon is h4-h5, to open the h-file.
6...e5 has been the main move as of late: 7.♘de2 h5, with a complex game ahead.
7.g4 ♗g7 8.♗e3 0-0!
I believe this is a very important move, and a somewhat counter-intuitive one, because one of the main appeals of the Dragadorf is that Black can delay castling for awhile to lessen the punch of h4-h5. But his problem is that it is very hard to get the move ...b7-b5 in otherwise.
Black would love to get 8...b5?! in, but he is too slow. White can get his kingside play going: 9.g5! ♘h5 10.♗e2! and the position somewhat resembles the game, but White has gained a lot of time by playing ♗f1-e2

instead of ♗f1-g2-f3 and avoided playing a2-a3. Black just looks worse to me, e.g. 10...e5 11.♘f5!.

9.♕d2
The straightforward 9.g5?! is not as effective now that Black's king has left the centre: 9...♘h5 10.♗e2 e5!, when Black has good counterplay, for instance after 11.♘f5 (11.♘b3 ♘f4 also gives Black good counterplay) 11...gxf5 12.♗xh5 f4 13.♗d2 ♕xg5 I prefer his position.
With 9.♗g2, White could have considered preventing ...b7-b5, but his bishop will be misplaced on g2 if he castles long, as Black can hope to use the c4-square.
9...b5!

10.♗g2?!
This is not a mistake per se, but I think if White is playing ♗e3 and ♕d2, the most consistent plan is to play a somewhat slower Yugoslav Attack and try to give mate on the h-file.
The main line of my analysis was 10.0-0-0 ♗b7 11.f3 ♘bd7 12.h4. Massive complications will arise shortly and I do not believe Black is worse, but White does have the basic plan of h4-h5 to give mate. It would be interesting to

see how this position fares in practical games in the future.

10...♗b7 11.a3?!

This feels too slow to me. I was not really planning on playing ...b4 next anyway.

11.0-0 ♘bd7 12.e5 dxe5 13.♗xb7 exd4 should be around equal.

11...♘bd7 12.g5?

And now already I think White is seriously worse. Black does not really mind his pawns becoming doubled on the h-file as White cannot open any lines on the kingside, and Black's bishops are extremely strong.

During the game I was expecting White to try to trade off my g7-bishop with 12.♗h6. Probably Black is a little better, but it is nothing too special just yet.

12...♘h5! Not fearing the doubled pawns. 12...♘e8? 13.h4 would give White exactly what he wanted. h4-h5 is coming.

13.♗f3 ♘e5 14.♗xh5

14...gxh5?! Definitely not a bad move, and I think Black is still better, but I missed a stronger option.

Of course I had considered the correct 14...♘c4!, but I was worried

Sam Shankland admitted that his play in Montevideo had been less convincing, but who is going to stop you if you're 'in the zone'?

about 15.♕e2, thinking that after ...gxh5, ♘f5 will follow. But I missed an incredibly nasty computer-like shot: 15...♘xb2!!.

ANALYSIS DIAGRAM

Black simply plays as if he is not a piece down and grabs the b2-pawn. White cannot hold onto his extra material. For example, 16.♗f3 is well met by 16...♕a5!, when White loses a piece.

15.0-0-0 Now that White's king has left e1, I realized that ♘f5 could be an idea, but planned accordingly.

Obviously, the immediate 15.♘f5? runs into 15...♘f3+.

15...♖c8!

Black develops a new piece and prevents ♘f5 tactically.

16.♔b1?

Also bad is 16.♘f5? ♘c4! 17.♕e2 ♘xb2! and White loses, e.g. 18.♘xg7 ♘xd1.

Or 16.f4? ♘c4 17.♕e1 ♕b6!, when ...b4 is coming and White will not last long.

In my opinion, the jump 16.♘d5! was the only way to offer any resistance, but White is still clearly worse. Black has several good moves but my plan during the game was the simple 16...e6 17.♘f6+ ♗xf6 18.gxf6 ♘xe4, when Black is much better (19.♖hg1+ ♗g6 20.♗h6 ♕xf6!), though at least White has some hope to make trouble on the dark squares on the kingside.

16...♖xc3!

I was very proud of myself for this decision. The ...♖xc3 sacrifice is a very common idea in the Sicilian, but it is quite rare when White is able to recapture with a piece! Normally a lot of Black's compensation comes from ruining White's pawn structure by forcing him to play b2xc3. Still, here it proves correct, as the e4-pawn will fall and Black's light-squared bishop will be the boss of the board.

17.♕xc3 ♗xe4

18.f3?! I think that 18.f4! was the only way to offer any real resistance, but White's position is still bad. My plan in the game was the simple 18...♘c4 when Black looks better to me. (The computer prefers to grab the material with 18...♗xh1, but I was pretty worried about an untimely ♘f5.)

The obvious move 18.♖he1 allows Black to show a very nice bind: 18...♘f3! 19.♖e2 ♕d7!. White can barely move, and Black has the very basic plan of ...♕d7xh3 and queening the h-pawn. Ironically, I think the

pawn is happier on h5 than it would be on g6 because it can become a passer very quickly, it leaves the g6-square for the bishop, and in some previous lines, White never had chances to play h4-h5 to open the kingside.

18...♘xf3 19.♖hf1 ♕d7 20.♕b3

20...♘e5! Keeping everything simple. White's rooks are no better than Black's minor pieces, so Black is more or less two pawns up.

21.♖f4 ♗g6 22.♖df1 e6!

Again, keeping it simple. Black had plenty of other good moves, but I saw no need to allow ♘d4-f5. White still has no counterplay.

23.♖f6

23...♖c8!

A testament to Black's bishops being better than White's rooks is that White offered his rook for a bishop, and Black did not take it! Black is ready to attack White's queenside.

24.♗c1 ♖c4!

Taking aim at the d4-knight. If it can

be removed from its post, c2 will fall next.

25.♕e3 After 25.♖6f4 ♘c6!, c2 is a point of conquest.

25...♕a7?! A small blemish on an otherwise great game, but it doesn't spoil much. Instead, 25...♘c6 was simple and strong. For some reason I did not like the looks of 26.♘f3 ♗xc2+ 27.♔a1 ♗g6 because of b3 followed by ♗b2, but this is pretty silly, as Black is obviously winning.

26.♘f5 Apparently I missed the resource 26.b3, but it would not have changed the outcome: 26...♖xd4 27.♖xg6! hxg6 28.c3 and White got more than he deserved, though his position still looks totally hopeless to me after 28...♘c6 29.cxd4 ♗xd4.

26...♕xe3 27.♘xe3

27...♖h4! Even into the endgame, Black's compensation is through the roof. He is now taking a third pawn, and making a passed h-pawn.

28.♖6f4 ♖xh3 29.a4

Understandably, White was desperate to create some kind of counterplay, as his rooks did not manage to get any open lines all game, but this only hastened his defeat.

29...h6! Black will get ...hxg5 in, and have four connected passed pawns.

30.axb5 After 30.gxh6 ♗xh6 White loses material.

30...axb5 31.♖b4

31...♘d3!

The final finesse. Black had other winning moves, but I like this one for its simplicity. The rest requires no comment.

32.cxd3 ♗xd3+ 33.♔a2 ♗xf1 34.♘xf1 ♖h1 35.♖f4 hxg5 36.♖f2 ♗d4 37.♘e3 ♖xf1 38.♗xd4 ♖xf2 39.♗xf2

39...h4 40.♔b3 f5 41.♔b4 h3
White resigned.

I think my play was quite sloppy in Uruguay on the whole, especially in the early-middle rounds, but I was very happy with this game. I felt I played extremely well to beat a very strong player with the black pieces to take a share of the lead head, and in a very aesthetically pleasing manner.

∎ ∎ ∎

Shankland's rise hasn't gone unnoticed, as his fan-base has grown with many Americans eager to follow and revel in his tournament adven-

Montevideo 2018

1	Samuel Shankland	IGM	USA	2717	9
2	Diego Flores	IGM	ARG	2614	8½
3	Pablo Salinas	IM	CHI	2463	8
4	Sandro Mareco	IGM	ARG	2643	8
5	Brian Escalante	IM	PER	2422	8
6	Jorge Cori	IGM	PER	2659	8
7	Kevin Cori	IM	PER	2468	8
8	Robert Hungaski	IGM	USA	2510	8
9	Emilio Cordova	IGM	PER	2621	8
10	Guillermo Vazquez	IM	PAR	2436	7½
11	Tomas Sosa	IM	ARG	2453	7½
12	Felipe El Debs	IGM	BRA	2537	7½
13	Jose Martinez	IGM	PER	2539	7½
14	Neuris Delgado	IGM	PAR	2613	7½
15	Cristhian Cruz	IGM	PER	2576	7½
16	Jeffery Xiong	IGM	USA	2656	7½
17	Sergey Erenburg	IGM	USA	2563	7½
18	Awonder Liang	IGM	USA	2571	7½
19	Diego di Berardino	IM	BRA	2525	7½
20	Alan Pichot	IGM	ARG	2564	7½
	167 players, 11 rounds				

tures. Barely days after his American Continental Championship success, the conquering hero returned home to receive a rousing reception by many of his hometown fans at the Mechanics' Chess Club in San Francisco, where, in front of a packed house – many of whom would have witnessed his first tournament at the club in 2004 as a precocious young teenager – he gave an entertaining and insightful lecture based around many of the key games en route to his triple triumph.

The big question many are now asking, is will Shankland's endeavours be rewarded with an invite into the elite arena? The initial chatter was a possible wildcard spot for the Grand Chess Tour US doubleheader in August: the Saint Louis Rapid & Blitz and/or Sinquefield Cup – but those spots went instead to the now Miami-based Cuban No.1, Leinier Dominguez, and World Champion Magnus Carlsen respectively. But fear not Shankland fans, as the ever-grinding rumour mill is heavily hinting that in the offing could well be an invite to the Tata Steel Masters in Wijk aan Zee in the early new year. ∎

FIDE ELECTIONS: A THREE-HORSE RACE

If a week is a long time in politics, then a month and a half – the interval between this article and my previous one – is an aeon. The grand change, of course, is that Kirsan Ilyumzhinov – the man whose 23-year reign in FIDE was defined by industrial-scale cronyism, corruption and cavalier disregard for the law – has finally been consigned to the trash-can of chess history, where he belongs. When the former Deputy Prime Minister of Russia, Arkady Dvorkovich, announced his candidacy for FIDE President, with not-so-subtly-disguised Kremlin support, it was obvious that the Kalmyk conman's time was up. Sure enough, shortly thereafter the bedraggled remnants of Kirsan's dwindling support-base were summoned to Moscow to be introduced to their new master. A beaming Lewis Ncube – Continental President for Africa – and the Belgian/Monegasque/Liechtensteiner hired-hand, Willy Iclicki, were perhaps the most familiar, if not distinguished, of this motley crew. In the published photographs, the normally radiant Kirsan cut a most forlorn and dejected figure.

I don't know too much about Dvorkovich, to be honest, beyond what I have read. I did meet his father – a well-known international arbiter – on a number of occasions, but that, of course, means little. What is certain is that he is a far more formidable opponent than the broken reed of a man he replaces. Naturally, he comes with full Russian diplomatic backing. One strongly suspects his campaign will not be devoid of substantial financial resources as well. This ought to be of concern to those who care about the independence of FIDE, although the cynic in me supposes that such people are few and far between. On the positive side, Dvorkovich is unlikely to have risen to such high political office without being at least reasonably intelligent (he is an economist by training), which gives one reason to hope for something other than the dissembling and air-headed claptrap to which we have long grown accustomed. Furthermore he is the Chairman of the Local Organising Committee of the 2018 FIFA World Cup – a hugely prestigious global sporting event, which is generally considered to be well-run. Clearly he possesses considerable talents. Last, but by no means least, Arkady Dvorkovich does not appear on any US sanctions list – an important point if FIDE ever desires to open a normal bank account again.

Talking of US sanctions, Georgios Makropoulos had previously announced Dr. 'Jaime Aguinaldo' (sic) as part of his 2018 election ticket. The former Angolan Finance Minister, Aguinaldo Jaime, has been a Vice President of FIDE for the past four years, so it may appear a little surprising to some that the Deputy President didn't know his name. In fact, it merely illustrates how FIDE is run by a small clique within a bloated Board of yes-men. A two-minute Google search shows that Dr. Jaime has been questioned by Human Rights Watch over the disappearance of $2.6 billion from the Angolan treasury, and appears extensively in a US Senate report 'Keeping Foreign Corruption Out of the United States: Four Case Histories'. The 80 pages of detailed accusations make entertaining reading. Literally minutes after I had tweeted this, Makro's great apologist of the moment, Malcolm Pein, replied that he would be removed from the ticket. Does this presage a brave new Makro world, thanks to clean Mr. Pein? Fat chance. Dr. Jaime has now been replaced by Zambian Health Minister, Dr. Chitalu Chilufya, who himself stands accused of massive corruption. He has not been convicted, but Chilufya's selection undoubtedly raises many questions. One can only conclude that Makro either does not know how to use a search engine, or he simply does not care about the company he keeps. Or both. Malcolm Pein is obviously not in charge (although he would very much like to have us all believe otherwise). And if he actually had 'zero tolerance' of corruption, as he ridiculously claimed in a recent Chess editorial, he would resign from the ticket forthwith.

In contrast, I am very happy with my own #cleanhands-4fide team. The first one to join – Lekan Adeyemi from Nigeria – ran for the African continental presidency in

'Last, but by no means least, Arkady Dvorkovich does not appear on any US sanctions list – an important point if FIDE ever desires to open a normal bank account again.'

2014, losing narrowly to the aforementioned Lewis Ncube, in Tromsø, in highly controversial circumstances, with intervention from Makro's minions. Votes were held in rival meetings in different rooms. To say that the outcome was acrimonious would be something of an understatement.

Nigeria is the most populous country in Africa and I greatly value Lekan for his loyalty. A while ago he informed me that four years ago, sometime before the election, he was offered a massive bribe ($100,000 initially, quickly rising to $200,000) to switch support to Kirsan. This proposal was made in his own country, by people you do not know, and cash was literally stacked upon the table in front of him. He turned it down. Lekan is a property developer, building stadia and the like, but that is a large sum of money by anyone's standards – particularly for a Nigerian. Incidentally, another person – a member of Kasparov's ticket – told me privately that he was offered a similar sum of money to switch to Kirsan in 2014. Either we have a couple of fantasists (other delegates tell similar tales – although involving much smaller sums), or Kirsan has some very unruly fans.

Paul Spiller, from New Zealand, is the President of the Oceania Chess Confederation. A quiet, softly spoken person, he is well-respected within his region. He is the first person from Oceania ever to appear on a FIDE ticket.

Ruth Haring, a WIM and former President of the USCF, adds a wealth of experience, knowledge and competence to our group. She will be General Secretary.

Lukasz Turlej, from Poland, will be my Deputy. I am delighted to have someone young (32), bright and energetic, representing an important country with a rich chess history, as my number 2.

Panu Laine, the former Finnish federation president, has a strong business background and will be my treasurer. I have got to know him, over green curries and beers, through his regular participation in the Thailand Open, which is organised by his fellow countryman Kai Tuorila.

FIDE is run on what I may term as the 'Makro model'. This involves extracting as much money as possible from the ordinary player. The one thing the Greek Chess Federation does really well is organising events like the World or European Youth Championships. These conveniently enough involve paying little or no financial prizes, with hundreds, or even thousands of people descending on hotels, off season. The heavily discounted room-rates ensure these tournaments are hugely profitable to the host country. Makro-FIDE is unrelenting at taxing titles – whether for

playing, organising, training or arbiting. The cost to busy federations, of rating tournaments, can run into many tens of thousands of euros every six months. This rent-seeking model suppresses activity, particularly in poorer federations, and thus guarantees that chess fails to reach anywhere near its full potential. The whole model must be inverted, with proper commercial sponsorship ensuring that funds are distributed from the centre outwards, not vice-versa.

I would like to see profound constitutional changes, including strict term-limits. It is a sick joke to see Makro now parading himself as the reform candidate when he has steadfastly opposed this vital change throughout his decades in power. Proxies – the way to guarantee a federation delivers after accepting a bribe – should be abolished immediately. Anyone familiar with FIDE procedures will know the dozens of votes cast in this manner have a grotesque bearing on the outcome of any election. Federations must conform to a bare governance minimum, having statutes, accounts and elections, before being recognised by FIDE. Currently many fail to do so. An independent outside

'One can only conclude that Makro either does not know how use a search engine, or he simply does not care about the company he keeps. Or both.'

commission, free from political interference, must pass judgment on these cases – not the disgracefully-biased body that does so now. And whilst we are at it, I would suggest that delegates must have at least a tenuous connection with the federation they represent. I very much doubt that Nikos Kalesis, the current delegate of the Solomon Islands, can even find the country on the map. If that is not a whoring of democracy, I do not know what is.

The reform wish-list goes on, such as introducing lengthy or even lifetime bans for cheats. However, none of this will happen unless delegates can recognise the once in a generation opportunity to elect clean leadership.

Nigel Short

Editorial note: The views that Nigel Short expresses in his column are his and do not reflect an editorial viewpoint.

Chess Pattern Recognition

ARTHUR VAN DE OUDEWEETERING

Who blinks first?

A common attacking tool is putting a knight *en prise*. But are you going to keep it there?

Here is a fairly basic example, stemming from the Steinitz Variation of the French Defence, a rich source for these steady knights in the attack:

Mateusz Bartel
Mihajlo Stojanovic
Zurich 2016

position after 15...h6

16.c3 White does not need to fear a capture on g5 right away: after 16....hxg5 17.hxg5 his queen will quickly reach the open h-file. But what's the text-move about? **16...d4?! 17.♗h7+** Without a doubt, 17.cxd4 hxg5!? 18.hxg5 ♘b4 or 17.♗xd4 ♘xd4 18.cxd4 ♗c6 was planned. 17.♗c2, though, seems as good as the intermediate check in the game. **17...♔f8 18.♗c2!** This was the idea of White's 16.c3. Having vacated c2 for the bishop, White can create a battery along the b1-h7 diagonal. Had Black moved his king to h8, the pawn on f7 would have been *en prise* now. **18...♕b5** Preventing ♕d2-d3. 18...dxe3 19.♕xd7 (and not 19.♕d3 ♘b4). **19.♗xd4 hxg5?** Black can't resist the tempta-

tion any longer and decides to take at last. He did overlook a typical tactical stroke, though... **20.hxg5 g6 21.♕f2 ♘xd4 22.♖h8+ ♔g7 23.♖h7+! ♔f8** 23...♔xh7 24.♕h4+ ♔g8 25.♖h1 is also end of story. Not an unusual or difficult combination; fair chance that some of you are reminded of the charming game Polgar-Berkes, Budapest 2003. **24.♕xd4 ♗a3** 24...♗c6 25.f5!, and the queen reaches the h-file: 25...gxf5 (25... exf5 26.e6) 26.♕h4. **25.b4** 1-0.

Here's another knight *en prise*. No need to retreat, but how can White support it and prove its sortie to be correct?

Dmitry Jakovenko
Vadim Zvjaginsev
Sochi 2015

position after 14...h6

15.b4! Now, after 15...♘xd3 16.♕xd3, the white queen has landed on the desired

diagonal: 16...♗xg5 (16...hxg5 17.hxg5 g6 18.♗f2 or 16...g6 17.♘xe6 are simply killing) 17.hxg5, and White is the first to break open the enemy kingside. 15...♘e4 16.♗xe4 does not work for Black either, so Black answered **15...♘a4 16.♘xa4 bxa4 17.♗h7+** 17.c3, as in the former game, to continue with ♗d3-c2, looks strong as well, but can be met by 17...a5!, when Black can also scupper White's plans on the diagonal b1-h7 with ...♗a6. **17...♔h8 18.♕d3**

Effectively putting the bishop on the road of no return! Now ♗g6 or ♗g8 must work for White, otherwise his pieces will be completely misplaced. Strong nerves and ditto calculating abilities are required here.

18...♗xg5 18...♗xb4 is not easy to refute at all. Jakovenko would have had to find 19.a3 ♗c5 (19...♗a5 20.♗g6), and only now 20.♗g8, for example: 20...f5 21.exf6 ♕b6+ 22.♔a2 ♘xf6 23.♖b1 ♕a7 24.♗xc5 ♕xc5 25.♖xb7, and White is clearly better. **19.hxg5 a5 20.b5 ♕e7 21.♗d4** 21.gxh6 can always be met by 21...g6. **21...♖fc8 22.c3 ♖ab8 23.♔a1 ♘c5 24.♕c2** Now the bishop may come back to d3, when White can start thinking about capturing on h6 again. Black's subsequent inventive defence could not save him (1-0, 39).

Sometimes the queen supports the knight in the attack from close by:

Remember Igor Ivanov's words:
'We Russians never go back.'

Ivan Cheparinov
Kiril Georgiev
Sunny Beach 2012

position after 13.♕h5

13...h6 Pushing the knight back, at least that's what Georgiev intended, of course. With hindsight, 13...♘h6! would have been better. This looks ugly after 14.♕xh6 gxh6, but not utterly bad, since 15.♘e6 can be met by 15...♘xe5!. **14.♘df3!** When a knight is being driven away from g5, remember Igor Ivanov's boastful words: 'We Russians never go back'. Of course, at the same time, always keep a cool head. Actually, the natural retreat 14.♘gf3 meets with the surprising 14...c4 15.♗xf5?! ♘c5 16.♗c2 ♘d3+ 17.♗xd3 cxd3 18.0-0 ♗f5, with decent compensation for the pawn. After the text-move White threatens 15.e6, followed by 16.♕g6. **14...b6** It is pretty amazing how much time White has to build up the attack, for example: 14...♕b6 15.e6 ♘f6 16.♕g6 ♗xe6 (16...hxg5 17.hxg5 ♕xe6+ 18.♔f1 ♕f7, and now 19.♘e5 works for White: 19...♕xg6 20.♘xg6, winning back the piece) 17.♘e5!, preparing ♘xe6 followed by ♗xf5 and ♗xh6. The text-move allows a much more sudden conclusion. **15.e6 ♘f6**

16.♕f7+ 16.♕g6 hxg5 17.hxg5 ♕xe6+ 18.♘e5 cxd4 19.♗f4 was also possible, but who could withstand the charm of 16.♕f7? **16...♖xf7 17.exf7+ ♔h8 18.♘e5** Threatening mate in one. White will remain at least an exchange up, although with his next move Cheparinov went chasing for the brilliancy prize and still ended an exchange up, winning the game. **18...g6 19.♘xg6+ ♔g7 20.♘xe7 ♕b7 21.♘g6 ♘bd7?** 21...♘fd7 would have vacated another square for the black king, when White's advantage seems to vanish. **22.♘e6+ ♔xg6 23.h5+ ♔xf7 24.♘d8+ ♔g7 25.♘xb7** (1-0, 34).

Of course the same can happen on the other side of the board:

Dragos Dumitrache
Arkadij Naiditsch
Mulhouse 2011

position after 14.a3

Well, there is not really a way back here, so Black develops, vacates the c-file for the rook and stops the pin along the d-file.
14...♗d7 15.exd5 What if White takes the knight? 15.axb4 axb4 16.♘xd5 ♗a4 was another idea behind Black's 14th. Play may continue with 17.♕c4 ♗xd1 18.♔xd1 ♖xd5 19.exd5 (19.♕xd5 ♕a5) 19...♖a1+ 20.♔c2 ♕d7, and Black's king is in deep trouble. **15...♗f5 16.♘d4?** Again the capture gives Black sufficient play: 16.axb4 axb4 17.♘a4 ♕a5 18.♗d3 (18.♘xc5 ♕xc5+ 19.♕c4 ♕a5) 18...♗xd3 19.♖xd3 ♕xa4 (19...♕b5!?). However, a much better way to parry the threat of 16...♗c2 was 16.♖d2. **16...♗xd4 17.♖xd4 ♕b6** Attacking the rook, at the

same time threatening 18...♘d3+. Now the black pieces swiftly gather around White's king. **18.♕d1 ♖fc8 19.♖c4 ♖xc4 20.♗xc4 ♖c8 21.axb4** Finally; but now it does not even win a piece. **21...♖xc4 22.♕e2 ♕xb4 23.♕e5 ♗g6 24.♖e1** 24.♕xf6 ♕b3 **24...♕a4** 0-1.

Be careful with your conclusions now, because appearances deceive. What do you think of the b4-knight in the following position?

Gelfand-Aronian
Dortmund 2006
position after 15.♔b1

15...a5 16.♘e5! Leaving the knight for what it is! Black has no evident way to back up the knight, which will present no danger on its own. So Gelfand just does his own thing on the other side of the board! 16.axb4 axb4 17.♘d5 ♗xd5 18.exd5 d6!? 19.♕xe7? ♖e8 20.♕xd6 ♕f5+ is one line, but why should White bother to consider these complications? **16...♖e8 17.♖he1 ♗f8 18.g4!** Getting started on the kingside. **18...g6 19.♗g3 ♖e6 20.f4 d6 21.♘xc6 ♘xc6** Finally the knight moves, but after **22.♘b5** White had built up a terrific position: more space, the bishop pair and centralized rooks. Gelfand wrapped it up nicely: **22...♘e8 23.e5 dxe5 24.♗d5 a4 25.fxe5 ♘g7 26.♕f3 ♖b8 27.♘d6 ♗xd6 28.exd6 ♘d4 29.♖xd4 ♖xe1+ 30.♗xe1 cxd4 31.♕xf7+ ♔h8 32.d7 ♕c5 33.♗b4** 1-0.

Don't be put off by some tension: these forward knights, even when under attack, can exert strong pressure. Yet even the bravest of knights needs support. ∎

Loving Leuven. Just like last year, Wesley So dominated the rapid part of the Your Next Move leg of the Grand Chess Tour, but this time he managed to defend his lead to finish overall first.

When Wesley starts winning

American rapid ace takes lead in Grand Chess Tour

The first two rapid & blitz legs of the 2018 Grand Chess Tour saw Wesley So in great shape. Both in Leuven and in Paris, the American was unstoppable in the rapid part. After two events So is leading the overall GCT standings ahead of Hikaru Nakamura, who won the trophy in Paris. **ANISH GIRI** reports.

The rapid and blitz tournaments in Leuven and Paris, both part of the Grand Chess Tour, have become regular fixtures on the calendar of elite events. Held for the third consecutive time, the format had not undergone any changes. What did change was that, for reasons connected to the football World Cup, the first leg of the GCT was not held in Paris this year, but in Leuven. Once again, the Top-9 of the Grand Chess Tour's 'universal rating system' and one 'wild card' crossed swords over the course of five days, with three days dedicated to rapid games, followed by two days of blitz. In Paris,

Vladimir Kramnik was the wild card, while I enjoyed this privilege in the Leuven leg.

Like all shows produced by the St. Louis Chess Club, the live broadcasts of the Grand Chess Tour are superb, and the chemistry between the commentators is getting better by the year. The organization is becoming smoother with every edition, too, and even the players (the majority anyway) are getting more accustomed to the somewhat obscure GCT specialty – the so-called 'delay' time-control, in which, in contrast to Fischer's increments, the time on the clock cannot be increased but only be stopped from decreasing.

Despite the fact that young talents are popping up all over the world, the top-10, no matter what selection process is going to be used, was made up of more or less the same players as before. Once again, we saw the familiar and beautiful faces that the chess fans are so happy to see. Since Magnus Carlsen has decided not to take part in the 2018 Grand Chess Tour (although he did accept the wild card for the Sinquefield Cup in August, the only 'classical' leg of the Tour), there was no clear favourite, and with quite a few rapid and blitz specialists around, it was hard to come up with predictions. It was likely that Fabiano Caruana and me (never famous for our blitz) and perhaps old hands Vishy Anand and Vladimir Kramnik would struggle, but as against that, I don't think too many people had expected Wesley So to do so well in the rapid parts in both Leuven and Paris.

One problem with rapid and blitz events is that there are so many games, spectacular ideas and over-sights that it is a challenge to just pick out the highlights. I had asked the editor to remove Nigel Short's column to create more space, but since this wasn't an option for some reason, we'll have to work with what we've got. I am sure some things will fall by the wayside, but I still hope to share the tastiest bits with my readers.

Wicked Wesley

There are many good adjectives to describe Wesley So's play in Leuven and Paris, but none of them begins with a 'w'. I really wanted to go for an alliteration here, however, so there you are. For most players, the first few rounds are crucial or even decisive, and Wesley is definitely one of them. So to understand his success and his domination in the rapid part, let's have a look at how it all started.

Fabiano Caruana
Wesley So
Leuven Rapid 2018 (1)

position after 28...cxd5

Wesley has equalized comfortably, but I am pretty sure he wouldn't have planned to win the game at this point, if Fabi had, like any ordinary person, taken with the rook.

29.exd5? Fabiano is not a child and does not need to be criticized like one, so I am sure he had reasons for committing this huge strategic error. But essentially this is just giving Wesley a great start with one terrible move. I know that Fabiano is a very

> **'Fabiano Caruana is a very strong player, who can be compared to a machine, but like all machines he has bugs sometimes.'**

strong player, who can be compared to a machine, but like all machines, even the most powerful ones, he has bugs sometimes.
29.♖xd5 is completely equal, if you ask me.

29...♗d6
I would even prefer the hyper-posi-tional 29...g6!? to take all control of the light squares on the kingside away from White, against which 30.h4 h5 31.g4 is no help: 31...♗xh4 32.gxh5 ♖b2, and Black is far ahead.

30.h4
If White had time for h4-h5 and ♗d3-♕e4, his risky decision would be justified, but he hasn't, since ...f5 comes quickly.
30...♕d7 31.♗d3 g6 32.g4 ♕e7 33.h5 ♕g5

And Wesley was ruthless in the conversion.
34.hxg6 fxg6 35.♕g2 ♖f8 36.♖e1 ♖b3 37.♖e3 ♖f4 38.♗f5 ♖b2 39.♗e6+ ♔g7 40.♖f1 ♖xc4 41.♕g3 ♖bb4 42.♕h2 ♖f4 43.♔h1 e4 44.f3 h5 45.♕h3 hxg4 46.♗xg4 ♖b8 47.♕g3 ♖h8+ 48.♔g2 ♖xg4
White resigned.

In the second round, Wesley So, as White, found himself in a difficult position after the opening.

Wesley So
Shakhriyar Mamedyarov
Leuven Rapid 2018 (2)

position after 24...h3!

Mamedyarov has taken the initia-tive, since the pawn on h3 is incred-ibly annoying and creates all sorts of disturbing mating nets.
25.♖ac2 ♘d5
25...♖d3! was the way forward. Black is on top.
26.♘e1 ♘b4 27.♖d2 ♖xd2 28.♕xd2 ♖a7 29.♕d7
In fact, Shakh has already messed it up, but here he had to forget his pride by all means.

29...♖a8? He should have played 29...f5! 30.♕xb5 ♖a2, with unclear play. **30.♕xh3** Now Wesley takes charge. **30...♘d3 31.♘xd3 ♕xd3 32.b4 ♕d2 33.♕f1 ♕xb4 34.♖b1 ♕c3 35.♖xb5 ♖a1 36.♕e8+ ♔h7 37.♖xa1 ♕xa1+ 38.♔g2 ♕f6 39.♕d7 c6 40.h4 g6 41.g4 ♔g8 42.g5 ♕c3 43.♕d8+ ♔h7 44.♕d4 ♕c2 45.♕f4 ♔g8 46.e4 c5 47.♕b8+ ♔h7 48.♕e8 ♔g7 49.♕e5+ ♔g8 50.♕d5**

After a stubborn defence Shakh was on his way to holding the game, but now he fails to spot the threat.

50...c4? 50...♕e2 was one of the moves that would hold. Black should

Tension in Leuven's Town Hall. Sergey Karjakin and Maxime Vachier-Lagrave blitz out their moves under the watchful eyes of Wesley So, Tony Rich (GCT organizer) and Anish Giri.

prevent h5, and eventually the c-pawn will provide enough counterplay. It is taboo here in view of ♕g4+, followed by an easy perpetual on squares d1 to g4. 50...♔g7!? also does it, with the idea 51.h5 gxh5.

51.h5!

Now it's over. **51...♕d3 52.hxg6** Black resigned.

After this 2/2 start (which, interestingly enough, mirrored his awful 0/2 start at the Candidates in Berlin, one of his worst events in recent times) Wesley began to feel at ease. The wide tables in Leuven facilitated his usual posture, and while his left hand, lost in the thick sleeve of an oversized Grand Chess Tour jacket, had found a comfortable spot west of the chess board, his right hand, in an equally thick sleeve, was throwing out strong moves at a fast rate. The loud, almost bell-like sound of the clock after each move usually meant bad news for his

Leuven rapid 2018		cat. XXII
		TPR
1 So	7	3001
2 Aronian	5½	2863
3 Vachier-Lagrave	5½	2860
4 Karjakin	5	2824
5 Nakamura	5	2825
6 Mamedyarov	4½	2778
7 Grischuk	4	2740
8 Caruana	3½	2697
9 Anand	2½	2617
10 Giri	2½	2615
9 rounds		

Leuven blitz 2018		cat. XXII
		TPR
1 Karjakin	11½	2883
2 Nakamura	11	2862
3 Vachier-Lagrave	10½	2837
4 Grischuk	9½	2804
5 Anand	9½	2804
6 Aronian	9½	2804
7 Mamedyarov	8	2735
8 So	8	2738
9 Caruana	6½	2675
10 Giri	6	2656
18 rounds		

Leuven combined 2018			
	rapid	blitz	total
1 So	7	8	22
2 Vachier-Lagrave	5½	10½	21½
3 Karjakin	5	11½	21½
4 Nakamura	5	11	21
5 Aronian	5½	9½	20½
6 Grischuk	4	9½	17½
7 Mamedyarov	4½	8	17
8 Anand	2½	9½	14½
9 Caruana	3½	6½	13½
10 Giri	2½	6	11
double points for rapid			

opponents. He went on to score a few more wins, one smoother than the other, for example this one.

Alexander Grischuk
Wesley So
Leuven Rapid 2018 (5)
Ruy Lopez, Berlin Defence

1.e4 e5 2.♘f3 ♘c6 3.♗b5 ♘f6 4.d3 ♗c5 5.c3 0-0 6.0-0 d6

Lines with ...d5 are very fashionable as well nowadays, but this has always been considered reliable.

7.h3 ♘e7 8.d4 ♗b6

9.♖e1

Karjakin tried 9.♗d3 later against So, with a similar position, except that White gets an extra option to play without ♖e1: 9...d5 10.♘xe5 ♘e4 11.♘d2 ♘d6 12.♘b3. This idea of sending the knight to c5 was introduced by Anand against Karjakin at the 2016 Candidates, but it has never looked too threatening. 12...f6 13.♘f3 ♗f5 14.♘c5 ♗xd3 15.♕xd3 ♖e8 16.♗f4 ♗xc5 17.dxc5 ♘e4 18.b4, and here you would probably need a couple of accurate moves, but Black should manage.

9...d5 10.♘xe5 ♘e4 11.♘d2 ♘d6 12.♗d3 f6 13.♘ef3 ♗f5 14.♘b3

As mentioned, this line is not the most dangerous one, but it is hard to imagine that White could lose here. Yet, with the wind behind Wesley and a risk-free black position, holding his opponent to a draw also proved too hard a challenge for Grischuk.

14...♗xd3 15.♕xd3 ♘g6 16.♘c5?!

This is not great, I think, because the knight doesn't do anything here, now that White is too late to tickle the d6-knight with ♗f4.

16...♖e8 17.♗d2 c6 18.b3 ♕c7 19.♖xe8+ ♖xe8 20.♖e1 ♖xe1+ 21.♘xe1 ♗xc5 22.dxc5 ♘e4 23.b4 ♘e5

Now Black is clearly doing well, although the position still feels tenable for White.

24.♕c2 ♘c4 25.♘f3 ♘cxd2
26.♘xd2 ♕e5

Wesley plays it most unpretentiously, but White apparently still has to be a bit accurate in the queen ending.
27.♘xe4 ♕xe4 28.♕d1 ♕c4
29.♕g4 ♕xg4 30.hxg4 ♔f7

31.♔f1?
The right way was 31.f4! f5 32.gxf5 ♔f6 33.♔f2 ♔xf5 34.♔f3 h5 35.g3, and White will not run out of moves on the queenside: a3, a4 and b5, and if Black goes ...a6, he has a5.
31...f5?
31...g6! was the right way for Black to get what he wanted: 32.♔e2 ♔g5 33.♔f3 f5 34.gxf5 h5.
32.gxf5 h5 33.♔e2 ♔f6

Holding Wesley So to a draw while the American enjoyed the benefits of a risk-free position proved too hard a challenge for Alexander Grischuk too.

34.♔e3?
34.f4 would be similar to the note above, when the game would be drawn: 34...♔xf5 35.♔f3 h4 (or 35...g5 36.fxg5 ♔xg5 37.g3 ♔f5 38.a3 ♔g5 39.♔f2 with a draw) 36.a3 g6 37.a4 g5 38.g4+! hxg3 (38...♔f6 39.f5) 39.fxg5. This is an important line, and not at all easy to calculate in a rapid game.
34...♔xf5 35.♔f3
Here White is completely lost. Black will eventually create an outside passed pawn, and the ♔e4-♔d3xc3 penetration will be deadly.
35...g6 36.a4 a6 37.g3 g5
38.g4+ hxg4+ 39.♔g3 ♔e4
40.♔xg4 ♔d3 41.♔xg5 ♔xc3
42.f4 d4 43.f5 d3 44.f6 d2 45.f7
d1♕ 46.f8♕

White did manage to queen at the same time, but the queen ending is hopeless.
46...♕g1+ 47.♔h6 ♕h2+
48.♔g6 ♕g3+ 49.♔h6 ♕h4+
50.♔g6 ♕g4+ 51.♔h6 ♕e6+
52.♔g7 ♕e5+ 53.♔g6 ♔xb4
54.♕f7 ♕g3+ 55.♔h6 ♕e3+
56.♔g7 ♕c3+ 57.♔h7 ♕c2+
58.♔h6 ♕c1+ 59.♔g7 ♕b2+
60.♔f8 ♕h8+ 61.♔e7 ♕e5+
62.♔f8 ♕xc5+ 63.♔g8 ♕d5
White resigned.

At the end of the rapid section, Wesley was two points ahead of his closest pursuer, which meant a really nice cushion, since the points from the rapid games counted double. This allowed him to coast to first place overall in the blitz section, which is exactly what he did, although not, as he himself admitted, without some help from the Lord.

Onto Paris

In Paris, a similar scenario unfolded, except that, after another strong start, the rapid-machine called Wesley experienced a brief malfunction.

Shakhriyar Mamedyarov
Wesley So
Paris Rapid 2018 (2)
Semi-Tarrasch

1.d4 ♘f6 2.c4 e6 3.♘f3 d5 4.♘c3 c5 5.cxd5 cxd4 6.♕xd4 exd5 7.e4 ♘c6 8.♗b5 dxe4 9.♕xd8+ ♔xd8 10.♘g5 ♗e6 11.0-0 ♗b4 12.♘cxe4 ♘xe4 13.♘xe4 ♔e7

14.♗xc6 14.♗e3 ♖hd8 15.♗xc6 bxc6 16.♖fc1 ♗d5 17.♗c5+ ♗xc5 18.♘xc5 was Mamedyarov-Karjakin from the 2016 Baku Olympiad. Karjakin ended up on the verge of losing, but I am sure that with some good work, either at home or at the board, this endgame can be held.

14...bxc6 15.♗e3 ♗d5 16.♗c5+
Shakh plays like he did against Karjakin, except that he forgot to start with 14.♗e3; but that's not too important.

16...♔d7? Wesley must have overlooked the following nuance: 16...♗xc5 17.♘xc5 is obviously almost identical to the endgame above.
17.♘f6+! gxf6 18.♗xb4

And this endgame is incredibly nasty. I am sure Wesley would have loved to be on the other side of this, but when he had to defend it, he showed himself to be human too, and Shakh finished it off quite smoothly. An opposite-coloured bishop ending with so many weak pawns

can probably only be held if Black can force both rooks off the board. And while one pair can be traded, the second pair will remain forever.
18...♖ae8 19.f3 ♖e2 20.♖f2 ♖he8 21.b3

21...f5?! 21...♖xf2! 22.♔xf2 ♖a8! was needed. Now Black can hope to improve his pawn structure on the queenside: 23.♗a5 c5, but of course the endgame is still extremely ugly.
22.♖d1 a6 23.♖d4 h5 24.♔f1 ♖xf2+ 25.♔xf2

This already looks lost for Black.
25...f6 26.♗c3 ♖a8 27.♖h4 ♗f7 28.♗xf6 c5 29.♖a4 ♔c6 30.♗c3

Paris rapid 2018		cat. XXII
		TPR
1 So	6	2907
2 Nakamura	5½	2863
3 Karjakin	5½	2862
4 Aronian	4½	2784
5 Vachier-Lagrave	4½	2781
6 Anand	4½	2784
7 Caruana	4	2735
8 Mamedyarov	3½	2699
9 Grischuk	3½	2704
10 Kramnik	3½	2701
9 rounds		

Paris blitz 2018		cat. XXII
		TPR
1 Nakamura	12	2908
2 Aronian	11	2864
3 Vachier-Lagrave	10½	2838
4 Karjakin	10½	2839
5 So	9	2782
6 Grischuk	9	2784
7 Mamedyarov	8½	2758
8 Anand	8	2741
9 Kramnik	6	2656
10 Caruana	5½	2637
18 rounds		

Paris combined 2018	rapid	blitz	total
1 Nakamura	5½	12	23
2 Karjakin	5½	10½	21½
3 So	6	9	21
4 Aronian	4½	11	20
5 Vachier-Lagrave	4½	10½	19½
6 Anand	4½	8	17
7 Grischuk	3½	9	16
8 Mamedyarov	3½	8½	15½
9 Caruana	4	5½	13½
10 Kramnik	3½	6	13
double points for rapid			

♔b5 31.h4 ♗e6 32.♖a5+ ♔b6
33.b4 cxb4 34.♗xb4 ♖c8 35.a3
♖c2+ 36.♔g3 ♖e2 37.♖c5 ♗d7
38.♖d5 ♔c7 39.♖d4 ♖e6 40.♖d2
♗b5 41.♔f4 ♖e2 42.♖xe2
♗xe2 43.♔g5 ♗f1 44.♔xh5
f4 45.♔g4 ♗xg2 46.h5 ♗f1
47.h6 ♗d3 48.♔g5 ♔c6 49.♔f6
♔d5 50.♔g7 ♗f5 51.♗d2 Black
resigned.

This didn't mean a definite end to
Wesley's streak, because he bounced
back with two great wins. Have a look
at this one.

Vladimir Kramnik
Wesley So
Paris Rapid 2018 (4)

position after 20.♕xd5

After a somewhat unsuccessful
opening, White is about to force a
queen swap and a draw. But now we
enter the stage of the game in which
Wesley thrives. There is no risk or
danger, so he can calmly calculate if
he might have a trick of his own.
20...♘c2! 21.♖d1 ♕e8!

22.♘b5?
After 22.♘e4! ♘xa3 23.♘d6 ♕c6

Vladimir Kramnik received the wild card for Paris, the city where he used to live before
he moved to Geneva. Dropping his queen sped up the Russian's loss to Wesley So.

24.♘xc8 ♕xc8 25.♕d7 White should
have sufficient counterplay, since he is
going to win an important pawn due
to the black knight being somewhat
offside.
22...♕e2! 23.♗c1?
23.♔g1 was the best move, but it costs
a pawn: 23...♘xa3 24.♘xa3 ♕xa2.
23...♗f8

There are too many threats.
24.♘xa7 ♖c5 25.♕f3 ♘e1+
26.♖xe1 ♕xe1 27.♗e3 ♖f5
28.♕a8 ♕a5 29.a4 ♖e5 30.♘c6?

Black was already winning, but
giving a queen was not necessary. 0-1.

At the end of the (third) day in Paris,
Wesley So once again found himself
at the top of the rapid standings. This
time, however, his lead was just one
point (meaning 2 points in blitz),
which proved to be insufficient with
18 rounds of blitz ahead. In the final
two blitzing days, he was overtaken
by Sergey Karjakin and the overall
winner in Paris, our next protagonist
Hikaru Nakamura.

At the venue of the Paris leg of the Grand Chess Tour there was no space for spectators, but there were live broadcasts in English, French and Russian.

Hardworking Hikaru

King's Indians, 1.e4 c5 2.♕h5, what could be more romantic? But Nakamura's romantic days are long gone. These days, it's all draws with the Berlin and the Queen's Gambit Declined, and even the name of our samurai 'Hikaru-Nakamura' merely means 'Shining-Middle of the Forest' and what exactly that means depends very much on which forest and how bright something shines. True, the American number 3 briefly toyed with the Sicilian Dragon recently, but that, too, only served to force perpetual check or get a tenable endgame. Such are the harsh realities of chess openings at the highest level these days. In Paris, Hikaru went through 27 games with just one loss and worked incredibly hard for his result. His rapid win against Fabiano Caruana was characteristic, albeit a bit too much so, even by his own standards.

Hikaru Nakamura
Fabiano Caruana
Paris 2018 (4)

position after 51.♘e2

The game could have ended here, since White will clearly be unable to win the e4-pawn without trading the knights (which would be a dead draw, since the bishops are of opposite colours), but in reality it only started.
51...♗b4 52.♘f4 ♔g8 53.♘h3 ♗f8 54.♘f4 ♗d6 55.♘h3 ♗f8 56.♔f1 ♗g7 57.♔e2 ♔f8 58.♔d2 ♔e7 59.♔c2 ♗h6 60.♔c3 ♔e6 61.♔d4 ♔f5 62.♘f4 ♗g7 63.♘h3 ♗h6 64.♔c4 ♔e5 65.♔c3 ♘g4

66.♔d2 f5 67.♗f1 ♔f6 68.♗b5 ♗f8 69.♔e2 ♗d6 70.♗f1 ♗e5 71.♔g2 ♗d6 72.♘g1 ♗e5 73.♘e2 ♔e7 74.♘c1 ♘f6 75.♘b3 ♘g4 76.♗e2 ♘f6 77.♘a5 ♗d6 78.♘c6+ ♔f7 79.♗c4+ ♔g7 80.♘d4 ♘g4 81.♗e2 ♘e5?

Nobody knows what Hikaru wanted with all his pointless manoeuvring, but it would be absolutely unfair to him to criticize him for this. After all,

our hard worker is being rewarded for the effort he has put into all this, now that Black sheds a pawn.

82.♗xh5! The funny thing is that this position must still be completely defensible, but Fabi still collapses.
82...♔f6 83.♗e2 ♗c5 84.♘b5 ♗b6 85.♘c3 ♗c5
85...♗a5, for example, would stop g4, but whatever.
86.g4 ♔e6 87.g5 ♗e7 88.♗d1 ♔f7 89.♘d5 ♗d6 90.h5

'Hikaru Nakamura's rapid win against Fabiano Caruana was characteristic, albeit a bit too much so, even by his own standards.'

90...gxh5?! With 90...♔g7! Black is in time to hold, thanks to counterplay against the g5-pawn.

91.♗xh5+ ♔g7 92.♘f4 ♘d3 93.♘e6+ ♔h7 94.♗e8

94...♘e5? 94...♗e5! was better, stopping the pawn a square further.

95.♘d4! ♗e7 96.♘xf5 ♗xg5 97.♘g3 ♔g4 98.♘f1 ♔g7

White was probably going to win a second pawn, but walking into another fork was unnecessary.

99.♗c6 ♘f6 100.♘g3 ♘g4 101.♗xe4

And the rest was easy (1-0, 123).

Let's look at one more rapid win by Hikaru.

Vishy Anand
Hikaru Nakamura
Paris Rapid 2018 (8)
Modern Defence

1.e4 d6 Hikaru encountered some problems in his ♖e1 Berlin, so he decided to switch to the good old Pirc against Vishy, which he had also used successfully against him in the blitz in Leuven, although he was rather fortunate there, too.

2.d4 g6 3.♘f3 ♗g7 4.♗c4 ♘f6 5.♕e2 0-0 6.0-0

6...♗g4

6...♘c6 is bad, as Izoria showed against Hikaru at the US Championship: 7.e5!.

7.c3 7.e5 is less deadly here: 7...dxe5 8.dxe5 ♘d5.

7...♘c6 8.h3 ♗xf3 9.♕xf3 e5 10.d5 ♘e7

Black gets a playable, King's Indian type of position.

11.♗d3 ♘d7 12.c4 f5 13.♕d1 c6!?

Opening the c-file is an interesting decision. It is always hard to judge whether Black should do so or not.

14.♘c3 cxd5 15.cxd5 ♔h8 16.♗e3 ♘g8 17.♖c1 a6 18.♖c2 ♗h6 19.♗xh6 ♘xh6 20.♕d2 f4 21.♖fc1 ♘g8 22.f3

At first I was a bit surprised by how Vishy handled the game here, but it does make some sense. He brings the knight to f2 to stop any ideas of ...g4 and wants to enjoy his c-file.

22...♘gf6 23.♘d1 a5 24.♘f2 ♘c5 25.♗b5

25.♖xc5!? was interesting.

25...♕b6?!

25...a4! was stronger, preventing White from stabilizing his b5-bishop.

26.♖xc5!

Vishy shows class here.

26...dxc5 27.a4 c4 28.♕c3

28.♖xc4 ♖ac8 29.b3 (29.♕c3!? also makes sense) 29...♖xc4 30.bxc4 was one other way of handling the c-file issue.

28...♕d6 29.♕xc4 ♖ac8

This was a must anyway.

30.♕xc8 ♖xc8 31.♖xc8+ ♔g7 32.♘d3

The position has become very hard to judge. On the one hand, White has a protected passer and can stop the queen from penetrating with ♘c5!. On the other, Black has a nasty dark-square route for his king on the queenside. Unclear.

32...♘h5 I am not really sure about

this move, but I assume Hikaru didn't realize that White would eventually send his king to the queenside. Interesting was 32...g5!?, with either ...h5/...g4 or – similarly to the game – ...♔g6-h5-h4.

33.♔f1 ♛b6 34.♞c5 ♔h6 35.♔e1

Garry Kasparov, one of the main movers of the Grand Chess Tour, visited both Leuven and Paris, always showing his unrelenting passion for the game whenever he sat down at the board.

35...♞g3? This is quite ridiculous, but again I guess Hikaru didn't yet understand who was going where at that point. It's never easy to figure out what's going on in such a mess, especially in a rapid game.

Best was 35...♔g5!. The king should go to g3 and the knight to f6, as happens later in the game. Black would be way faster and the position is unclear.

36.♔d1 ♔h5

36...♝f1!? is quite desperate: 37.♝xf1 ♛xb2 38.♞d3, and White is on top.

37.♔c2 ♔h4 38.♔b1 ♞h5

39.♔a2? Wasting a crucial tempo. Instead, 39.♞b3!, planning ♜c2-♜d2, would have crowned Vishy's concept. I guess he was afraid of a check on g1, but that didn't work: 39...♛g1+ 40.♔a2!. It's important to keep the rook active. 40...♛xg2 41.d6 ♞f6 42.♜f8!, and of course White

will never trade the d-pawn for the knight. He is completely winning: 42...♛g5 43.♞xa5 etc. The a-pawn will soon start running, too.

39...♔g3

Now Black is back in business.

40.♞d3 ♛d4! 41.♜c2 ♞f6 42.♞c5 ♛d1 43.♔b3 g5 44.♞d3

44...♞d7? 44...h5, followed by ...g4, would have kept things unclear.

45.♔c3 45.d6!. **45...♞b6?**

45...♛g1! leads to a draw: 46.♝xd7 ♛d4+ 47.♔d2 ♛e3+ 48.♔c3.

46.♞xe5? 46.d6! would just win; there is no stopping d7: 46...♛g1 47.♜f2!. **46...♛e1+**

47.♔b3? Vishy collapses. 47.♜d2 was totally fine for White, since Black would have to force a draw.

47...♛b4+ 48.♔a2 ♞xa4 49.♝xa4 ♛xa4+ 50.♔b1 ♛d4 51.♞c4 a4 52.d6 ♛d1+ 53.♜c1 ♛d3+ 54.♜c2 b5 55.♞d2 b4 56.♔c1 b3 57.♜c3 ♛xd6

White resigned.

Hikaru Nakamura's blitz games will be dissected by Maxim Dlugy in his Blitz Whisperer column, so I am sure that whatever scepticism I have expressed as regards Hikaru will be amply compensated for elsewhere in this issue.

Lyrical Levon

Obviously, it wasn't only the Americans who provided highlights. Both Maxime Vachier-Lagrave and Sergey Karjakin fought for the top spots in both events, and while Levon Aronian remained in their shadow, I noticed a lot of carefree and relaxed play on his part. Many of his games were crowned with straightforward mating attacks. I know, because in three of them I was at the receiving end. Here is one against Fabiano Caruana.

Fabiano Caruana
Levon Aronian
Leuven Rapid 2018 (8)
Ruy Lopez, Berlin Defence

1.e4 e5 2.♘f3 ♘c6 3.♗b5 ♘f6 4.d3 ♗c5 5.c3 d5 6.♘bd2 0-0 7.0-0 dxe4 8.dxe4 a5 9.a4 ♕e7 10.h3 ♘e8 11.♖e1 ♘d6 12.♗d3 ♗e6 13.♘f1 f6 14.♗e3 ♗xe3 15.♘xe3 ♕f7 16.♕e2 ♖fd8

17.♖ed1 ♘e7 18.h4 ♘ec8 19.♗c2 ♘b6 20.♘d2 ♘bc4 21.♘dxc4 ♘xc4

22.♘d5?
Amazing, but the mistake here is

almost identical to the one Fabi made against So in the first round! Talking about #chesspatternrecognition.
22...♗xd5 23.exd5 ♘d6

Now watch the train rolling in.
24.c4 b6 25.♖a3 f5
With the support of the eternal knight on d6 and the major pieces from behind, the e- and f-pawns are poised to start running down the board.
26.♖c3 e4 27.c5 bxc5 28.♖xc5 ♖e8 29.♖c1 ♖e7 30.♗d1 f4 31.♕e1 f3 32.♖1c3 ♖f8

Full harmony in Black's forces.
33.♕f1 ♕g6 34.♔h2 ♕g4 35.♖xc7 ♕xh4+ 36.♔g1 ♖e5
Massacre! 0-1.

Vigilant Vidit

Finally, I can't finish this tale without mentioning a small incident that unsettled the GMs in Leuven on the first day. My friend and colleague Vidit Gujrathi is yet to find his social media identity, so he attempted to go viral by posting the following fragment:

Karjakin-Grischuk
Leuven Rapid 2018 (2)
position after 34.d4

Commenting: 'I simply can't believe that Grischuk didn't play ♕g2 here. So elementary! #GrandChessTour.'

The tweet did receive a couple of likes and retweets and maybe even gained the Indian superstar a few more followers. However, Levon Aronian decided to use his own account (rumours say he occasionally uses the account of his dog, 'Ponchik', to share his frustrations with the twitter sphere) to respond immediately with: 'Almost like missing mate in 1...'

Perhaps a subtle reference to the mate in one Vidit walked into in his game against Robert Hovhannisyan in Lake Sevan, 2015?

And later, already past midnight, Sergey Karjakin, who seemed to have trouble falling asleep, chipped in as well: 'Almost like missing stalemate!'

With the addition of the following diagram, which shows the final position of Vidit's game against Gelfand (Black) in this year's Poikovsky tournament:

Lessons to be learned. ∎

SECRETS OF OPENING SURPRISES

A surprise against a popular Anti-Grünfeld

Jeroen Bosch

4...e5!?

'Black more or less refutes White's 4.b4 move order.'

As the Grünfeld continues to set 1.d4 players serious opening problems, many players seek to avoid this 'Hyper-modern' weapon. By the way, it was in Vienna 1922 that Ernst Grünfeld introduced his opening by defeating Alekhine. I have often been struck by the fact that 1922 is hailed as a sacred year in English Modernist literature with the publication of both *The Waste Land* (T.S. Eliot) and *Ulysses* (James Joyce), and I do not consider this to be a mere coincidence...

Some players use Réti or English move orders to circumvent the Grünfeld. In my previous column, we looked at another way of avoiding the Grünfeld: 1.d4 ♘f6 2.♘f3 g6 3.♘c3 and so on. For a few years already, top players have been using 1.d4 ♘f6 2.c4 g6 3.♘f3 ♗g7 4.e3!? – most notably in Caruana-Carlsen, Karlsruhe/Baden-Baden 2018! The point of this move order is that 4...d5 would allow 5.cxd5 ♘xd5 6.e4, when the absence of a knight on c3 more than makes up for the tempo. Of course, in a King's Indian the early 4.e3 is a concession, but apparently entering the theoretical ramifications of the Grünfeld is worse!

Another way to avoid the Grünfeld is 1.d4 ♘f6 2.♘f3 g6 3.♘bd2!?, which has also been used by the modern greats of the chess world (often in rapid and blitz games). Although developing the queen's knight to the passive square d2 is a concession too, it also has its merits. In

reply to a King's Indian set-up White will play e2-e4 and c2-c3, strengthening his centre, while the 'Grünfeld move' 3...d5 is met by an early b2-b4 to gain space on the queenside. If it were not for this latter advance, 3.♘bd2 would be fairly insipid and passive.

In short, there is nothing really wrong with 3.♘bd2 and it could easily have been an SOS subject for White, but it isn't! The reason is that I want to share with you the game Nabaty-Safarli from the European Championship in Batumi early this year. In that game, Safarli's wonderful fourth move seems to defuse an important move order for White.

Tamir Nabaty
Eltaj Safarli
Batumi 2018

1.d4 ♘f6 2.♘f3 g6 3.♘bd2 d5

Stopping White from setting up the ideal pawn centre, and avoiding typical Pirc or King's Indian type of positions. Let's have a brief look at how play might develop after 3...♗g7 4.e4 d6.

Now White has to make up his mind about his king's bishop:

■ 5.♗d3 0-0 6.0-0 ♘c6

Let's see two Carlsen efforts:
– 7.♖e1 e5 8.c3 h6 (the immediate 8...♘h5 deserves attention) 9.♘f1 ♘h5 10.♘e3 ♘f6 (the point of the pawn sacrifice is 10...exd4 11.cxd4 ♘xd4 12.♘xd4 ♗xd4, and now 13.♘f5!) 11.♗c2 ♖e8 12.d5 ♘e7 13.c4 was an edge for White in a typical King's Indian position, Carlsen-Radjabov, Moscow 2010.
– 7.c3 ♗d7 (7...e5 8.dxe5 ♘xe5 9.♘xe5 dxe5 10.♘c4 ♕e7 11.♕e2 ♖d8 12.♗g5 h6 13.♗h4 b6 14.♖fd1 ♗b7 15.♘e3±, Xiong-Shankland, St. Louis 2018) 8.♖e1 e5 9.dxe5 ♘xe5 10.♘xe5 dxe5 11.♘f3 ♕e7 12.h3 ♖fd8 13.♕c2 is a typical position that is about equal, Carlsen-Vachier-Lagrave, Paris 2016.
■ 5.♗c4 0-0 6.0-0 ♘c6 (or 6...♘xe4 7.♘xe4 d5 8.♗d3 dxe4 9.♗xe4 ♘d7 10.c3 c5, as in Vitiugov-Dubov, St. Petersburg 2017) 7.c3 e5 8.dxe5 ♘xe5 (8...dxe5±) 9.♘xe5 dxe5 10.♖e1 ♗d7 11.♗f1 ♗c6 12.f3 ♕e7 13.♘c4

The position is equal here, but Black's next move is too weakening: 13...b5?! 14.♘a5 ♗d7 15.b4 c5 16.a3 ♖fc8 17.♗e3 ♗f8 18.♘b7 cxb4 19.cxb4 ♗c6 20.♘a5±, Rakhmanov-Smirin, Khanty-Mansiysk 2013.

■ As an afterthought, please note that Nabaty and Dubov have played the subtle (or, depending on your viewpoint, 'over-sophisticated') 5.♗b5+!? to avoid Black's best set-up with ...♘c6 and ...e5.
Let's return to 3...d5.

4.b4!? This is a fairly recent trend. White is gaining space first before developing his kingside.
The natural 4.e3 has occurred far more often. After 4...♗g7 White can still go 5.b4, possibly followed by 5...0-0 6.♗b2 ♗f5

7.c4 (White can also develop the kingside first: 7.♗e2 ♘bd7 8.0-0 c6 9.a4 ♘e4 10.c4 ♖e8 11.cxd5 cxd5 12.♘xe4 ♗xe4 13.♕b3, and White had a typical annoying edge in the internet blitz game So-Vachier-Lagrave, chess.com 2017) 7...c6 8.♗e2 ♘bd7 (perhaps 8...a5 9.bxa5 ♕xa5 10.0-0 ♘bd7, as in Gelfand-Gupta, Gibraltar 2018, is preferable) 9.0-0 dxc4 10.♘xc4 ♘b6 11.♘a5,

with a slight edge in Carlsen-Vachier-Lagrave, Moscow blitz 2010.
It is telling that Grünfeld expert Peter Svidler has always chosen to avoid 5.b4 in reply to 4.e3:

■ 4...a5 5.c4 ♗g7 6.b3 0-0 7.♗b2 a4 8.♗e2 ♘f5 9.0-0 ♘bd7 10.b4?! a3 11.♗c3 dxc4 12.♘xc4 ♘e4, and Black had decent counterplay in Yu Yangyi-Svidler, Shenzhen 2017.
■ and most recently he played 4...♘c6 5.b3 ♗g7 6.♗b2 0-0 7.♗e2 a5 8.a3 b6 9.0-0 e6 10.c4 ♘e7 11.cxd5 exd5 12.b4 c6, with a tense middlegame in So-Svidler, Wijk aan Zee 2018.
So we may conclude that after 4.e3 White may not be able to get his favourite b2-b4 move in, which is why it makes sense to execute this advance on move 4.

Black now nearly always plays 4...♗g7 5.e3 0-0, and this transposes to 4.e3 ♗g7 5.b4, but White has managed to prevent (Svidler's) anti-b4 moves.
A creative try after 4.b4 is 4...e6, however, 5.a3 ♗g7 6.♗b2 0-0 7.e3 c6 8.c4 a5 nevertheless led to just the sort of game that White was seeking all along in Dubov-Ragger, Germany 2018.

Yet another way to try to gain something from the early 4.b4 is 4...a5, but after 5.b5 ♗g7 6.e3 c5 7.bxc6 bxc6 (7...♘xc6 8.♗b5) 8.♗a3 0-0 9.♗e2 ♗a6 10.0-0 ♖e8 11.♖b1 ♕c8 12.c4 White had a very pleasant game in Saric-Krstic, Mali Losinj 2017.

Safarli now comes up with a real shocker!

4...e5!?N

A fantastic move! If this works – and I believe it does – then Black more or less refutes White's 4.b4 move order.

5.dxe5 Clearly the only way to go, since 5.♘xe5 ♗xb4 6.e3 0-0 is very comfortable for Black.

5...♘e4

This active move was Black's intention. The pawn on b4 is hanging and White has to go for a very concrete game. Imagine his discomfort, just as he was ready to execute a series of mechanical moves (e3, ♗e2, 0-0, c4, ♗b2, in no particular order)!

6.♘xe4 The most natural move, I guess, although from now on, pawn b4 will be hanging with check. Here, however, White did have a choice, and it is necessary to examine the alternatives:

– Note that 6.a3?? ♘c3 blunders a queen!

– Black is also doing well after 6.♗b2?! ♗xb4 7.e6?! (7.c3 ♗xc3 8.♗xc3 ♘xc3 9.♕c2 ♘e4∓) 7...♘c3 (7...0-0) 8.exf7+ ♔xf7 9.♕c1 ♖e8, with an excellent game.

– It looks bad to play 6.c4?!, because of 6...♗xb4, but 7.♕b3 is actually a bit tricky. Strongest now is 7...♘c6, with the point that 8.cxd5

can be met by 8...♘c5 9.♕c4 b5!, and Black is better – after 10.♕xb5? ♕xd5 his advantage even increases.

Apart from Nabaty's 6.♘xe4, the moves 6.♗a3 and 6.c3 deserve some further scrutiny:

■ 6.♗a3 looks artificial, but remember that White is still a pawn up and ahead in development, while the Black knight on e4 is also hanging in the air. 6...♘d7! (6...♗f5 7.e3; 6...♘xd2 7.♕xd2 a5 8.e3 axb4 9.♗xb4±) 7.♘xe4 (Black has nothing to worry about after either 7.e3 ♗g7, or 7.c4 ♘xd2 8.♕xd2 ♘b6!, with excellent counterplay) 7...dxe4 8.♕d4!? (8.e6?! fxe6 9.♕d4 is comfortably met by 9...♕f6!) 8...exf3 9.e6

The point of White's play, but Black is fine after 9...♖g8 10.exd7+ ♕xd7 (Black has to take more care after 10...♔xd7 11.0-0-0 ♗e6 12.♕e4), and now White is the one who has to play accurately: 11.0-0-0 (11.♗e3+ ♕e6 12.exf3 a5∓) 11...♕xd4 12.♖xd4 fxe2 13.♗xe2 a5, and White ought to keep things within drawing margins.

■ Black doesn't need to be unduly worried either after 6.c3, although you are well-advised to look at the following forcing sequence. 6...♘xc3 7.♕b3 ♘e4 8.♘xe4 (8.♗b2 ♗e6; 8.e3 ♗g7; 8.a3!? ♗e7! – but not 8...♗g7? 9.♘xe4 dxe4 10.♗g5!, and White's chances are to be preferred) 8...dxe4

and now it's necessary to look at both the bishop and the knight sallies to g5:

– 9.♗g5 ♗e7 10.♖d1 ♗d7 (but not 10...♘d7? 11.e6!+−) 11.e6 fxe6 12.♗xe7 ♕xe7, and Black is at least OK after 13.♘d2 ♗c6.

– 9.♘g5 ♕e7 10.♘xe4 (10.a3 ♗g7) 10...♕xb4+ 11.♕xb4 ♗xb4+ 12.♗d2 ♗xd2+ 13.♔xd2 ♘d7, and now 14.f4 is objectively equal, although Black's position may have more long-term perspective.

6...dxe4 7.♕xd8+ ♔xd8

And now both the knight and the b-pawn are hanging.

8.♗g5+ White is a pawn up after 8.♘g5 ♗xb4+ 9.♗d2 ♗xd2+ 10.♔xd2 ♔e7 11.♘xe4.

However, Black has easy development and a better structure, which means that he is fine after 11...♖d8+ 12.♔c3 (Black has good counterplay after 12.♔e3 ♘c6 13.f4 ♘b4) 12...♖d5!? 13.f4 ♗f5! 14.♘f6 (14.♘g3 ♖c5+ 15.♔d2 ♖xc2+ 16.♔d1! keeps it even. Note that after 15.♔d4 ♘a6! 16.♘xf5+ gxf5 White is in some danger) 14...♖c5+ 15.♔d4 ♖xc2 – this is a sharp endgame in which both sides have chances.

We should also investigate 8.♘d2 ♗xb4 9.♗b2, when Black does best to saddle White with an Irish pawn centre: 9...e3! 10.fxe3

and now many moves promise Black a decent game: 10...♗e6 (10...♗xd2+ 11.♔xd2 ♗e6; 10...♔e7) 11.0-0-0 ♔e7.

8...♗e7 Not 8...♔e8? 9.0-0-0, when Black has to play 9...♗e7 after all.

9.0-0-0+

White can also keep his king in the centre with 9.♖d1+ ♘d7 10.♗xe7+ ♔xe7 11.♘g5.

Here, too, Black has many ways to reach a good game. Note that pawn a2 is often weak and that the pawn on b4 provides Black with a nice 'hook' to obtain play along the a-file. 11...♘xe5 (11...e3!? is perhaps best, keeping ...a5 in reserve as well and obstructing White's development; also good is 11...a5!? 12.b5 ♘c5) 12.♘xe4 ♗e6.

There is something to be said for keeping the white rook on a1 to protect the a-pawn. Nevertheless, White certainly has no edge after 9.♗xe7+ ♔xe7 10.♘g5 (10.♘d2 ♗f5 – or the immediate 10...e3 – 11.g4 ♗xg4 12.♗g2 e3!; 10.♘d4 ♖d8 11.e3 ♘d7 is even) 10...♗f5 11.g4 (11.f3 h6) 11...♗xg4 12.♘xe4 ♘c6, and Black retrieves the pawn with a decent game.

9...♘d7 10.♗xe7+

Black is up for preference after 10.e6?! fxe6 11.♗xe7+ ♔xe7 12.♘d2 (or 12.♘g5 ♘f6 13.f3 ♗d7∓) 12...a5 (also good is 12...e3 13.fxe3 ♘e5∓) 13.b5 ♘c5. White must really watch his step here.

10...♔xe7 11.♘g5

Other moves are worse: 11.♘d4 ♘xe5 12.e3∓, and 11.♘d2 e3! 12.fxe3 a5 13.b5 ♘xe5∓.

11...♘xe5

Safarli must have considered other moves, too. Black is more than fine after both 11...a5 12.b5 e3 and 11...e3 12.f4 a5 13.b5 ♘c5.

It is clear by now that the audacious 4...e5 has been fully vindicated by the subsequent play.

12.♘xe4 c6

Black also has sufficient compensation for the pawn after 12...♗e6! 13.a3 a5 14.b5 f5 15.♘c5 ♗g4 16.♘d3 ♗c4. This time I would avoid 12...a5?!, which gives White at least some play after 13.b5 (13.♖d5!?) 13...♗e6 14.f4.

13.e3 b5!

Planning ...a5.

14.f4

White more or less forces the draw, as otherwise he might even be in danger. Despite his extra pawn, White has nothing after 14.a3 a5 15.♗e2 axb4 16.axb4 ♗e6, for example: 17.♘c5 ♗c4! 18.♗xc4 ♘xc4, and Black has counterplay, as witness 19.♖d7+ ♔f6 20.♔b1 ♖a3 21.♖hd1 ♖ha8 22.♘b3 ♖a2.

14...♘g4

15.h3 Here 15.♖e1?! a5! favours Black.

15...♘xe3 16.♖e1 ♘xf1 17.♘c5+ ♔f6 18.♖hxf1 a5 19.a3

And a draw was agreed in Nabaty-Safarli, Batumi 2018.

In conclusion, we have seen that after 4.e3 Black may – à la Svidler – try and prevent b2-b4 altogether, while 4.b4 can be met by Safarli's bold 4...e5!, when Black gets excellent compensation for his sacrificed pawn. ∎

Naka's Magic

In the first two legs of the Grand Chess Tour, Hikaru Nakamura once again displayed his extraordinary Blitz skills. In the rapid & blitz spectacle in Leuven, he came second in the blitz part, behind Sergey Karjakin, while in Paris the American's first place in the Blitz brought him overall victory. **MAXIM DLUGY** explains why Nakamura is so good at Blitz.

When playing Blitz, it's very important to have some magic tricks up your sleeve that you unleash when your opponent least expects them. Since the time to react is quite limited, chances of success increase significantly. Hikaru Nakamura's Blitz performance in Leuven and Paris, the first two legs of the 2018 Grand Chess Tour, was extremely impressive. The American boasted a whopping combined score of 23/36, with Sergey Karjakin, another Blitz superstar, faring only slightly worse at 22/36 points.

The magic that 'Naka' used in his Blitz games included surprisingly early opening traps in his beloved 1.b3 system, excellent tactical traps set against his opponents' most natural moves and, of course, amazing resourcefulness in lost positions.

Furthermore, he displayed his outstanding ability to force his opponents to solve difficult tactical problems, which many of them failed to do even in seriously winning positions.

We'll watch the blitz magician in action and see what we can learn from his games. Of course, in order to be able to carry off all these magic tricks, every good magician has to use speed as his main resource. And one thing is for certain – Hikaru knows how to stay ahead on time!

In the following game against Anish Giri, Hikaru uncorked a cool tactical trick which, quite miraculously, he went on to use successfully against Wesley So and Shakhriyar Mamedyarov in the same event as well, gaining a huge advantage in a few moves.

Hikaru Nakamura
Anish Giri
Leuven Blitz 2018 (10)
East-Indian Defence
1.♘f3 ♘f6 2.b3
Here we go. As I wrote in a previous

article in New In Chess 2018/3, which focused on the b3 system used by both Hikaru Nakamura and Sergey Karjakin, knowing your specialty blitz opening systems is more important than their objective strength. We'll find further evidence here.
2...g6 3.♗b2 ♗g7 4.e3 0-0 5.d4 c5

It's quite reasonable to try and exchange the c-pawn for the d-pawn, and it certainly looks as if Black is very comfortable here. So the next two white moves should have come as a surprise.
6.dxc5 ♕a5+ 7.c3!
Quite an unpleasant surprise! As it turns out, the natural 7...♕xc5 can now be met by 8.♗a3!, and Black has to sacrifice the e-pawn. But will he get sufficient compensation?

7...♖e8

Anish decides to save the e-pawn, but allows Hikaru to hold on to his extra c-pawn. Wesley So and Shakhriyar Mamedyarov also fell into this trap, but opted to shed the e-pawn instead. They both lost. Here's how they continued:

7...♛xc5 8.♗a3 ♛b6 (Nakamura-So saw 8...♛c7 9.♗xe7 ♖e8 10.♗xf6 ♗xf6 11.♘d4 ♗c6 12.♗e2 d5 13.0-0 ♘e5 14.♛d2 ♗d7 15.♘a3 ♖ac8 16.♖ac1 a6 17.♖fd1 ♛a5 18.♛b2, with nebulous compensation for the pawn) 9.♗xe7 ♖e8 10.♗xf6 ♗xf6 11.♗e2 ♘c6 12.0-0 a5 13.♘d4, with no real compensation for the pawn in Nakamura-Mamedyarov.

8.b4 ♛c7 9.c4

The bishop opens up, and Black is simply a pawn down.

9...a5 10.a3 axb4 11.axb4 ♖xa1 12.♗xa1 ♘a6 13.♗e5 d6 14.cxd6 exd6 15.♗c3 ♘h5 16.♗xg7 ♘xg7 17.b5 ♛a5+ 18.♘bd2 ♘c5 19.♗e2 ♘e4 20.0-0 ♘c3 21.♛e1 ♘e6

22.♘e4!

Hikaru rarely misses such tactical shots.

Hikaru Nakamura knows that a myriad of factors play a role in Blitz, but to begin with it's just great fun.

22...♘xe2+ 23.♛xe2

And the soon-to-be-combined efforts of White's knight and queen were too much for Anish, who preferred to resign rather than see the queen go to b2.

Nakamura's resilience in the most difficult positions is amazing. Many of his opponents mysteriously lose their cool and start dropping pieces. The reason is, of course, quite simple. They are always behind on time, and instead on focusing on the *coup de grâce*, they start playing impulsively, allowing Hikaru to take over. Let's take a look at a typical tactical skirmish that ends in Naka's favour.

Shakhriyar Mamedyarov
Hikaru Nakamura
Paris Blitz 2018 (17)
Queen's Pawn Game

1.d4 ♘f6 2.♘f3 e6 3.e3 c5 4.♗d3 d5 5.b3 ♘c6 6.0-0 ♗e7 7.♗b2 0-0 8.♘bd2 b6 9.a3 ♗b7 10.♛e2 ♛c7 11.♖ac1 ♖ac8 12.c4 dxc4 13.bxc4 cxd4 14.exd4 ♖fe8 15.♖fe1 ♛b8 16.♘e4

White is slightly better, but Black has a number of defensive ideas at his disposal.

16...♘a5?! Hikaru's choice is extremely provocative. As White is clearly planning to attack on the kingside, it looks safer to play 16...♘xe4 17.♛xe4 g6 when, after 18.♛e3 ♗f6 19.h4 ♘e7, Black should have a fine position.

17.♘eg5! Shakh lives for initiative, so he is very happy to start piling up pieces on the kingside.

17...♛f4

'It looked like Hikaru would have to outdo David Copperfield to survive, but he did more.'

18.♘xe6!? An excellent intuitive sacrifice for a blitz game, which took White 32 seconds to play. What would you play in this position? It's interesting that although Hikaru felt there were choices to consider in this position, he didn't find the best moves in the 60 seconds he had allotted himself for his reply.

18...fxe6 In fact, Black would have done best not to accept the Greek gift with 18...♕h6! 19.♘eg5 ♗d6 20.♕f1 ♗f4!, with a good position.

19.♕xe6+ ♔h8 20.♘e5 ♗f8

This is a clear invitation to a draw, and while I was watching this game live, I wondered if Shakh would just go for the perpetual with ♘f7+/♘h6+. Forty-one seconds later, Shakhriyar put on his boxing gloves and played the best move:

21.♕h3! ♔g8 Now, how does White continue his attack?

22.♘d7??

Not like this! The time-pressure takes its toll and Naka emerges victorious from a very shabby position. White's 24 seconds were not enough to spot the more or less obvious 22.♗f5!, with some very serious threats. Even after the sternest defence 22...

h6 23.♘g6 ♕g5 24.f4 ♕h5 25.♖xe8 ♖xe8 26.♗e6+ ♔h7 27.♕xh5 ♘xh5 28.♗f7 ♘xf4 29.♘xf4 White would be pretty happy with an extra pawn in the endgame.

22...♘e4! The knights part company, since Black covers the h7-square. It's game over!

23.f3 ♘g5 24.♕h5

24...♖e3

This will do, but 24...♖xe1+ 25.♖xe1 ♕d2 would be lights out even faster.

25.♘e5 ♖xd3 26.♘xd3 ♕f5 27.d5 ♘xc4 28.♗a1 ♗xd5 29.♔h1 ♖c6 30.♘f2 ♕g6 31.♕g4 ♘e3 32.♖xc6 ♘xg4 33.♖xg6 ♘xf2+

White resigned.

In the next game, it looked as if Hikaru would have to outperform David Copperfield to survive, but he did more: he came back to win a completely lost position against one of the greatest players of all

time, who happens to hold the title of World Rapid Champion. Here's how he did it.

Vishy Anand
Hikaru Nakamura
Leuven Blitz 2018 (15)
Modern Defence

1.e4 d6 2.d4 g6 3.♘c3 ♗g7

Hikaru loves playing the Modern or the Pirc Defence in blitz, because the dynamic counter-chances that these opening systems provide fully compensate for the lack of space that White needs to nurture to sustain an advantage. One inaccuracy that is natural to expect in a blitz game is often sufficient for Black to take over the initiative. This makes any g7-bishop fianchetto opening a decent choice for blitz.

4.f4 a6 5.♘f3 b5 6.♗d3 ♘d7

This system, delaying the development of the g8-knight till Black creates some counter-chances against the centre, has been taken up by Caruana, Kamsky, Adhiban and other strong grandmasters.

7.a4 Anand varies from his game against Fabiano Caruana, in which he played the immediate e5 and went on to lose a tough blitz game four years ago, when he missed mate in one after achieving a winning position.

7...b4 8.♘e2 c5 9.c3 ♗b7 10.0-0 ♘gf6 11.e5 ♘d5

12.♗d2 This simple developing move is a novelty. White has tried 12.e6, without much success, while another logical continuation, 12.c4 ♘c7 13.exd6 exd6 14.f5, would give Black reasonable equalizing chances after 14...♗xf3 15.♖xf3 cxd4 16.♗f4 ♘e5 17.♖h3 g5 18.♗xe5 ♗xe5.

12...bxc3 13.bxc3 cxd4 14.cxd4 0-0

Black has been unable to switch on his g7-bishop, so it seems logical to create attacking chances on the kingside with ♘g5. Vishy decides to place more pieces closer to Black's king before starting a direct assault.

15.♘g3 a5! One of the things that make Nakamura a great blitz player is his ability to quickly find moves to improve his position. The move ...a5, establishing a possible outpost for the d5-knight on b4, opening the a6-square for the bishop and, more importantly, preventing a5, took him all of four seconds!

16.♔h1 ♘b4

Objectively, Black has already solved his opening problems and should have roughly even chances in this position.

17.♗e4 d5 18.♗b1 ♗a6 19.♖e1 e6

20.f5!

Vishy, the old fox, senses that the position shows all the signs of a static meltdown in which Black will soon start infiltrating his queenside, and correctly sacrifices material to change the flow of the game.

20...exf5 21.♘xf5 gxf5 22.♗xf5

I suggest you stop to consider Black's options and time yourself to find the best defensive more here. After 61 seconds, Hikaru produced:

22...h6! Another nice defensive idea, which would probably be favoured by Vlad Kramnik, who loves to unbalance the position, would be 22...♘d3!, the main idea being 23.♗g5 ♗xf5 24.♗xd8 ♖axd8, with a very messy middlegame with equal chances.

23.♖a3

Stop to decide on Black's best defence now. Time yourself again.

23...♗c8!

The best move once again, which took Hikaru a whopping 42 seconds. Black threatens either ...♘b6 or ...♘xe5, neutralizing White's dangerous bishop. Now it's almost impossible to find the best continuation for White in a blitz setting. Moves like ♘h4, ♗b1 and ♖f1 are regarded highly by the engine, but who is going to play them?

24.♘g5?! Vishy intuitively sacrifices another piece. The line 24.♘h4 ♕xh4 25.♖h3 ♕xd4 26.♖g3 ♘xe5 27.♖xg7+ ♔h8 28.♖h7+ is a nice possibility offered by the engine.

Now ask yourself: Would you take the piece in a blitz game?

24...♘b6

According to our silicon friend, capturing was clearly the best option. Naka spent 24 seconds and decided to trust Vishy, who was clearly having a macho moment here. If you weren't afraid of the attack after 24...hxg5 25.♕h5, because you had noticed the reply 25...♘f6!! 26.exf6 ♗xf5 27.fxg7 ♔xg7 28.♗xg5 ♖h8!, and you did it in under a minute, well, then you are not human. In a tournament game, this variation could be worked out by strong masters looking for the right defence, but in a blitz game I don't think so!

25.♗h7+

The second best move. Computing power reveals that after the beautiful build-up move 25.♕g4, Black should not take on g5 in view of ♖h3, but after 25...♘c6 26.e6 ♖a7 27.♖h3 ♘xd4 28.♖xh6 fxe6 29.♗h7+ ♔h8 30.♖h4! White's attack becomes decisive.

25...♔h8 26.♕h5?

Not the best. Loading the diagonal with 26.♗b1 would give White a strong position. Still, this move forced Hikaru to use up almost all of his remaining time, as he sank into thought for 59 seconds before producing:

26...f6??

This move loses, while the beginner's fork 26...♘c4 would have given Black a nearly winning position.

It's interesting to note that gobbling up your opponent's pieces is quite often the best defence in a position in which things are beginning to look quite bleak. I can sympathize with Hikaru's instincts. He easily gives up material for the initiative, and here too, he probably just decided against giving White an extra move for a mere piece. Still, the bishop is quite a serious attacker here, and getting rid of it would go a long way.

Vishy would have to find the very unlikely 27.♘e6!!. I can't give three exclams in my database program; otherwise I would have. Amazingly, Black has nothing better than a draw after 27...♗xe6 28.♗xh6 ♘xa3 29.♖e3!! ♕c8!!.

ANALYSIS DIAGRAM

The end of Naka's last Blitz game in Paris. From a minus-5 position on move 46, Hikaru Nakamura managed to 'convert' against Fabiano Caruana to a win on move 122.

The only move to stay in the game since Black's hordes of material can now be sacrificed on g4 to prevent mate. 30.♗xg7+ ♔xg7 31.♖g3+ ♗g4 32.♖xg4+ ♕xg4 33.♕xg4+ ♔xh7 34.♕h5+, with perpetual check and a draw. Now many roads lead home and Vishy chooses one of them.

27.exf6

The now familiar 27.♘e6! would crush through immediately after 27...♗xe6 28.♗xh6 ♖f7 29.♗g6 ♖aa7 30.♗g5+ ♔g8 31.exf6 ♗xf6 32.♖g3, and Black can resign, even though White is down two pieces.

27...♕xf6

Amazingly, Vishy was almost two minutes ahead on time in a completely

winning position at this point. Here we begin to witness Hikaru's magic: with his back to the wall and spending a maximum of three seconds per move, he manages to survive and then win a losing position against Anand!

28.♖f3 ♗g4

The only defensive technique available in such positions is to try to meet White's queen with tempo, while developing your key defensive pieces. Naka gives up a bishop, just to win a tempo.

29.♕xg4 ♕xd4

30.♘f7+ 30.♗f4 was stronger, but this should do.

**30...♔xh7 31.♕f5+ ♔g8
32.♘xh6+ ♔h8 33.♘f7+ ♔g8**

34.♘h6+ ♔h8 35.♘f7+ ♔g8 36.♗c3!

It's no joke playing Vishy: he finds the move that should be enough to win the game.

36...♕xc3 Hikaru uses his last chance and gives up his queen. Otherwise, after 36...♕h4 37.g3 ♕h7 38.♕e6 ♖ae8 39.♘h6+ ♔h8 40.♕xe8, White will mate.

37.♖xc3 ♖xf7

Unfortunately for Vishy, he had used up his extra time looking for 36.♗c3, and now he has to play Hikaru with only a handful of seconds on his clock. White's decisive advantage is based, not on the piece count, but on Black's weak king. After pinning Black's bishop with a queen move on the g-file, White would be in full control, ready to start advancing his h- and g-pawns to finish the game.

But Vishy blunders, forgetting about his rook on c3.

38.♕e6? ♗xc3 39.♖f1?

Truly, it never rains but it pours. White could have kept the game going in a balanced complicated position with the intermediate check 39.♕g6+ ♗g7 40.♕xb6, with a fighting position.

39...♖af8

Now the game is over, as Black has a full house on his hands.

40.g4 ♘d7 41.g5 ♘c5 42.♕g6+ ♗g7 43.♖xf7 ♖xf7 44.h4 ♘bd3 45.h5 ♘f4 46.♕c6 ♘e4 47.h6 ♗f8 48.g6

48...♖f6 Naka is not afraid of ghosts. The pawns are useless.

49.h7+ ♔h8

And White resigned, probably noticing he will get mated in exactly 18 moves ☺.

In the last round of the Paris event, Hikaru just needed half a point to secure first place. As Hikaru was getting thoroughly and instructively outplayed by Fabiano Caruana, Sergey Karjakin, who was a point behind, quickly drew with Mamedyarov, guaranteeing Naka the tournament win. But Nakamura's game was not over yet...

We pick up the game after Black's 45th move to demonstrate another one of Hikaru's magic tricks: tenacity in technically lost positions.

Hikaru Nakamura
Fabiano Caruana
Paris Blitz 2018 (18)

position after 45...♘xd4

46.♖b1

The engine now suggests simply pushing the c-pawn till it queens, with an initial valuation of plus-5 for Black. Fabi wants to keep everything together and attempts to stop all counterplay instead. Curiously, this allows White to keep pestering Black until it becomes difficult to win.

46...♘b5? 47.♗e2 ♘d6 48.♖b6 ♖c3 49.♖a6 ♖c5 50.f3

Black's attempt to keep it all together cost him 3.7 pawns, according to the engines, and Black now really needs to conceive a plan to win the game.

'This game is a demonstration of another one of Hikaru's magic tricks: tenacity in technically lost positions.'

50...♔e7

An inaccuracy. 50...g6, getting rid of White's h-pawn, was important in order for Black to be able to afford leaving less stuff on the kingside and move his king towards the other side.

51.♖a7+ ♔f6 52.h6

Active defending.

52...gxh6 53.♗d3

53...♖c3 It would have been better to use the h-pawn to deflect White's rook: 53...h5!.

54.♔d2 ♖a3

This manoeuvre, leaving the c-pawn undefended, is just wrong.

55.♖a6 ♖a2+ 56.♔e1

56.♔e3 would have been way stronger here, but perhaps Hikaru was afraid of some mating themes; they don't seem to work, though.

56...♖g2

Caruana fails to push any of his passed pawns. After 56...a4 57.♖xc6 ♔e7 58.♖c7+ ♔e6 59.♖xh7 a3 60.♖xh6+ ♔e7 61.♖h7+ ♘f7 62.♗xf5 ♖a1+ 63.♔d2 a2 Black wins handily.

57.♖xc6 ♔e7 58.♖c7+ ♔e6 59.♖xh7 ♘f7 60.♗b5

'By maintaining a significant time advantage on the clock, he forces his opponents to make mistakes.'

The position is now roughly equal, which basically means that Hikaru is playing for the win.

60...♖xg3 61.♗e8 ♘d6 62.♔f2 ♖h3 63.♗c6

Hikaru senses Fabi's weakness and plays for maximum chaotic effect, forcing Black to consume his last seconds. Instead, 63.♔g2 would have led to an equal position.

63...d4?

63...♘c4 would have been very strong now; but no time left to think clearly.

64.♔g2 ♖h4 65.♔g3 ♖h1 66.♔g2

66...♖a1? After 66...♖c1!, attacking the bishop, Black is still winning.

67.♖xh6+ ♔e7 68.♖h7+ ♔f8 69.♖d7 ♘c4 70.♖xd4 ♖c1

And 72 moves later Hikaru 'converted' his extra time in this equal position to a win. (1-0, 122)

The above examples show us that Hikaru's Blitz prowess stems from a number of factors:

1 Excellent knowledge of the specialty opening systems he uses mostly for Blitz.

2 Incredible resourcefulness in bad positions.

3 Maintaining a significant time advantage on the clock, which forces his opponents to make mistakes.

And what's very important:

4 The ability to make reasonable moves at incredible speed when he is extremely low on time while trying to defend a bad position.

This last ability stands above all the rest, since it makes beating Naka extremely difficult. There is basically no easy way to beat this Blitz Magician! ∎

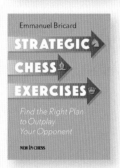

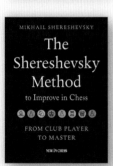
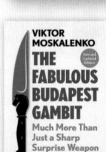
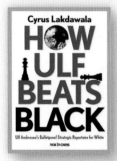

Judit Polgar

Tactical creativity

To sharpen your tactical acumen, you should study classical examples and try and solve puzzles – if only, as **JUDIT POLGAR** explains, because they may inspire you to create new tactical ideas yourself.

Tactics and combinations reflect the beautiful, artistic side of chess and offer the player's imagination a wide territory in which to manifest itself. It is also one of the most intensively examined territories in chess. Countless books with tactical puzzles have been published all through the history of the game, and players from all generations have enjoyed solving them. This obviously complicates matters when you are striving for 100% creativity. No matter how beautiful a combination is, there is a big chance that it contains elements from earlier ones that at some point were seen by the new combination's author.

As a kid I used to solve chess puzzles together with my sisters on a daily basis and over the years I have accumulated a 'tactical culture' consisting of over 50,000 combinations and studies. This helped me to quickly spot beautiful ideas over the board, but, as I already suggested, creating something completely new is much harder.

Over the years I have accumulated a 'tactical culture' consisting of over 50,000 combinations and studies.

It was gratifying, of course, to defeat a World Champion with a double bishop sacrifice, as I did in the following game:

Judit Polgar
Anatoly Karpov
Hoogeveen 2003

position after 24...♕c5

After **25.♗xh7+ ♔xh7 26.♕h5+** Black resigned, as after 26...♔g8, 27.♗xg7 will follow. But I had known this pattern since I was eight, when I saw the first example of this combination in the famous game Lasker-Bauer, Amsterdam 1889.

One of the first mating patterns we learn is based on the weakness of the back rank. Sometimes things may happen along the a- or h-file, but I believe that combining the two the way I did in the following example is really original, or at least very rare.

Jonathan Tisdall
Judit Polgar
Reykjavik 1988

position after 29.♔a2

Although my pieces are quite active and White's king is somewhat exposed, it doesn't look very likely that White might end up in trouble. But I spotted the possibility of gradually constructing an unexpected mating net.
29...♕d7 30.♘d2 ♖h4
My opponent must have noticed that my pieces are trying to take control of

the a4-square, but it is not yet clear in which way this could be dangerous for him.

To be honest, when I played my last move I was already hoping for the game continuation:

31.♘f3? Trying to get some relief by exchanging the central knight.

31...♘xf3 32.♕xf3 ♖1h3!
The rook temporarily relinquishes control of the back rank in order to cut off the white king along the third.
33.♕e2

33...♕a4!+
What a shock! After 34.♖xa4 ♖xa4+ 35.♔b1 ♖h1+ the rook closes the deadly net around the king. 0-1.

You can imagine what a feeling it was to finish the tournament in this way! I remember being completely ecstatic! The final position and the preceding manoeuvre are pretty unusual and I hope they are enjoyable for the reader.

■ ■ ■

The following game also features a strongly modified version of popular attacking patterns and is one of my favourites. It was published in New

In Chess 2003/4 with my full notes, so I will restrict myself to some general comments related to our theme.

Judit Polgar
Ferenc Berkes
Budapest 2003

position after 11...h6

In this kind of position, the well-known pattern involves h2-h4, inviting Black to open the h-file with ...hxg5. Many people thought that the game continuation was the fruit of home preparation, but in actual fact I was already on my own. Only later did I find out that a few earlier games had seen 12.h4, without any particular success for White.

12.♗h7+ ♔h8 13.♗e4 This manoeuvre is natural, but it involves a small tactical nuance.

13...hxg5?

Since 14.♗xa8 allows 14...g4, followed by ...♗g5, Black wins material. What's worse, I do not seem to be able to open the h-file. Or am I?!

14.g4!!
A quiet move, blocking the g-pawn in order to open the h-file with h2-h4. Berkes told me that he had seen it, but simply could not believe my attack

would be strong enough to compensate for the piece.

However, my intuition proved right. On the kingside I simply have a material superiority, since the a8-rook and the c8-bishop will find it hard to join the defence.

14...♖b8 15.h4 g6 16.hxg5+ ♔g7 17.♕f4 ♗b7

Black has played a series of logical defensive moves, but the rhythm is now broken by a typical combination:

18.♖h7+!
Speeding up the queen transfer to the h-file.

18...♔xh7 19.♕h2+ ♔g8
Or, if 19...♔g7 then 20.♕h6+ ♔g8 21.♗xg6 also wins.

20.♖h1 ♗xg5+ 21.♘xg5 ♕xg5+

22.f4 ♕xf4+ 23.♕xf4 ♗xe4 24.♕xe4 1-0. It is curious that we both saw the creative and completely original idea based on g4 in this game, but my opponent's sense of danger let him down.

■ ■ ■

I am particularly proud of two queen moves that were at the very least unusual in the following game.

**Judit Polgar
Laurent Fressinet**
Istanbul Olympiad 2000

position after 20...♔f8

I started my attack with the obvious
21.♖xd6 g6
But now there is no obvious way to continue the attack, as the king prepares to escape to g7. Even today I am still very proud of my next move:
22.♕c5!

This paradoxical self-pinning move attacks e5, preventing the king's intended evacuation. The pin actually works both ways to some extent, since 22...♕xa2? would run into 23.♖d8!+. The rook is obviously taboo due to 23.♕xd6+, followed by a series of checks retrieving the material with interest.
22...♔g8? An excusable mistake, since my 27th move was not easy to foresee. During the game we both considered that after 22...♖d4! (apparently the only saving move) 23.♕xe5 ♕d2+ 24.♔b1 ♗xd6 25.♕xh8+ ♔e7 Black's king would be relatively safe, which would make the final outcome uncertain.
23.♕xe5 ♗xd6 24.♕xd6 ♖c4
Preparing to restore Black's coordination with 25...♕c7.

My opponent must have thought I had nothing better than forcing a draw...

25.♕b8+ ♔g7 26.♕e5+ ♔g8
My opponent must have thought I had nothing better than forcing a draw, but I repeated moves only to get closer to the time-control. In better positions, this has long been considered a professional approach.

27.♕f6!!
I found this second mysterious queen move after understanding that the natural continuations would fail to win: if 27.♖d1 ♕c7 28.♕f6 ♕f4+ 29.♔b1 ♕xf6!, there would be no intermediate back rank check available.
At the end of this line, the rook would stand better on e1, but after 27.♖e1 Black has 27...♖c5!, driving my queen away from the central square on account of my hanging rook.
The move I played in the game, which I found after thinking for more than 30 minutes, changes the move order of the final attack. The queen is needed on f6 anyway and I can decide on which file to activate the rook. The move is creative in the sense that it ignores the first intuitive impulse that suggests an immediate activation of the rook.
27...♕c7 A familiar regrouping threatening 28...♕f4+.
27...♕xa2 would allow the alternative rook move: 28.♖d1 ♕a1+ 29.♔d2 ♕a5+ 30.♔e3, winning.

28.♖e1! The reason why this square is the best one now is obvious from my comment to 27.♕f6.
28...♕c6 With the rook on e1, 28...♕f4+ fails to save the game due to 29.♔b1! ♕xf6 30.♖e8+! ♔g7 31.gxf6+ ♔xf6 32.♖xh8, and now, e.g., 32...h5 33.♗c8, and Black cannot gain a tempo for his counterattack by attacking the bishop.
29.♗e6! Not the only winning move, since my domination was very clear already, but humanly the most convincing one.

29...fxe6
Played after 17 minutes. Black could not make much of a difference already.
The pawn ending arising after the long simplifying variation 29...♖xc2+ 30.♔b1 ♖c1+ 31.♖xc1 ♕xe6 32.♕xe6 fxe6 33.♖c8+ ♔g7 34.♖xh8 ♔xh8 35.♔c2 ♔g7 36.♔d3 ♔f7 37.♔e4 ♔e7 38.♔e5 is winning, since I have plenty of reserve tempi, enabling my king to get to either f6 or d6 in short order.
30.♖d1 Black resigned.

Tips
■ Pattern knowledge is important to gain self-confidence.
■ Far from restricting your creativity, it can actually inspire it. ■

MAXIMize
your Tactics
with Maxim Notkin

Find the best move in the positions below

Solutions on page 105

1. White to play

2. Black to play

3. White to play

4. White to play

5. Black to play

6. White to play

7. White to play

8. White to play

9. White to play

Pawns: Handle with care

US Champion Sam Shankland wrote a masterful book on pawns and our reviewer loved it. And it wasn't the only new book **MATTHEW SADLER** was pleasantly surprised by.

With the 4NCL in May (that long ago!), my playing activities for the coming six months have come to an end, so it's full focus on work from now on. Don't ask me why, but people always decide to go live with my projects in the summer months. Thank goodness there are chess books to keep my attention just a little bit on chess, or chess would get squeezed out completely.

As always, I'm keener on middle-game books than opening books and this month, I have been truly well rewarded for my good behaviour!

We start off with *Small Steps to Giant Improvement – Master Pawn Play in Chess* by Sam Shankland (Quality Chess). Only 26, Shankland recently became American Champion (perhaps the toughest national title on the planet!) and sailed past 2700 in the process (his rating soaring to 2727 thanks to further exploits described in this issue).

The book is a beautifully produced hardback of 331 pages, aimed at improving the reader's understanding of pawn play, and anchored around the simple observation that pawns cannot move backwards. I will confess that I rolled my eyes a little when I saw the title of the first chapter – 'Pawns Can't Move Backwards'. I'm a busy man, were we just going to waste time talking about the completely obvious? But as so often in this book, Shankland has an original way of demonstrating this difference between pawns and pieces in a memorable way:

'Pawns are the most punishing chessmen on the board. When you move a piece to a bad square and realize your mistake, you can undo it later in the game. Like in the following famous example:'

Judit Polgar
Garry Kasparov
Linares 1994

position after 36.♘d2

In this excellent position, Garry famously first placed the knight to c5 (which would allow the nasty fork 37.♗c6) and then – noticing the fork – moved it to the only other avail-

able square: f8. It's not a move he would ever normally have thought of – let alone played – but at least it doesn't lose the exchange.
36...♘f8 37.♘e4 ♘8d7

As Shankland points out: 'Kasparov understood that ...♘d7-f8 was deeply undesirable, but due to the touch move rule, he had no choice. Now he corrects the error! If you put a piece on a bad square, there is no rule saying that you cannot admit your mistake and bring the piece right back where it came from. The cost of two tempos is significant and Kasparov did lose a lot of time, but he ultimately won the game.'

Shankland then compares this to one of his own painful experiences with an incautious pawn move:

Sam Shankland
Georg Meier
Biel 2012

position after 56...♕h2

57.f5 After this move, an easy draw was turned into a tricky exercise of calculation which White was

Small Steps to Giant Improvement by Sam Shankland Quality Chess, 2018
★★★★★

Under the Surface by Jan Markos Quality Chess, 2018
★★★★★

correspondence chess. One particularly interesting chapter is an interview with Roman Chytilek, the world's highest-rated correspondence player.

It's difficult choosing one out of so many riches to share with you. However, I think that I'll show you something from the chapter 'Walking without Moving, Progress without Change'. We'll start with a bit from the introduction: 'Recently I have managed – entirely by chance – to make a major discovery that surely rewrites the history of chess. There are

not able to deal with in time pressure. White blundered the f-pawn and the game shortly after **57...♕g1 58.♕d2 ♕f1+ 59.♔e4 ♕c4+ 60.♔e3 ♕c5+ 61.♔f3 ♕xf5+ 62.♔g2 ♕g5 63.♕d7 ♕g4** 0-1.

Shankland: 'Like Kasparov, I put my chessman on a worse square than the one it came from. The key difference was that mine was a pawn! I immediately found myself wishing to slide the pawn back to f4, but the damage had been done and there was no reversing it. Given that a poor pawn move will generally cause more problems than a poor piece move, I decided to use this book to discuss the art of pawn play.'

Along the way, Shankland formulates a series of guidelines for avoiding mistakes like 57.f5. My opinion about these guidelines varies from day to day as they do skirt the fine line between good guidance and too-obvious-to-mention. For example: 'When deciding to advance a pawn beyond the fourth rank, you must decide if it is safe. The first part of this decision-making progress is to ask if any other pawns can protect it.' Extremely obvious and yet... a good heuristic! Shankland wins me over by illustrating these guidelines beautifully, for example by examining similar positions with slight differences (for example, in one position, White has a pawn on h3 stopping ...♞g4 and in the other he doesn't) and deducing further guidelines from this. I read this book every morning for about 20 minutes at breakfast for a few weeks and since then I have noticed that the thought 'oh, I'd really want my pawn back there' has become a constant companion during analysis! All in all, an excellent, original book!

■ ■ ■

The fun continues with Jan Markos' *Under the Surface* (Quality Chess). I didn't know the author's name at all (my shortcoming of course!), which always makes me just a little suspicious and reluctant when you receive such a book. 'Touch is read' in my

house, so you must be careful what you pick up! I can say however that I am not sorry I took the plunge: this is an incredibly creative book. I don't think that I have ever read a chess book that read more like a detective novel, in the sense that I never knew what the next chapter would bring! Markos has a host of original ideas about all sorts of chess topics and a wonderfully witty and enthusiastic way of bringing them across.

You just need to read the chapter titles to get a sense of the book: 'Three Faces of a Piece', 'Understanding the Beast', 'Anatoly Karpov's Billiard Balls', 'The Secret Life of Rooks', 'The Freezer', 'Looking for a Move, No Commitments', 'What Rybka Couldn't Tell You and Fritz Didn't Know'. As you can tell, the scope of the book is extremely broad: Markos draws in experiences and knowledge from pretty much every chess-related field: his own games, classic games, studies, computer chess – there are four fascinating chapters devoted to this subject – and, last but not least,

secret societies and fraternities in the world of chess, not unlike the Freemasons or the believers in the Holy Grail'. Markos introduces the secret chess sect: the 'Moveless Movers'. And he starts with this example:

Jan Timman
Vladimir Kramnik
Riga 1995

position after 9...b6

10.♘f6+ ♔f8 11.♘e4
After his 11th move, Timman's pieces are on the same squares as on the 9th move. And yet his position has improved (as Black cannot castle)!

'Shankland wins me over by illustrating these guidelines beautifully. All in all, an excellent, original book!'

Markos initiates also Peter Leko, Ludek Pachmann and Aron Nimzowitsch into this secret fraternity, as well as Vishy Anand. I loved this example:

Anatoly Karpov
Vishy Anand
Brussels 1991 (6th match game)

position after 18.♖fe1

18...♖dc8 19.♕b1 ♗b4 20.♗d2 ♖d8 21.a3 ♗c5 22.♘a4 ♗d6 23.♘c3

As Markos says: 'Did Black move at all? His pieces are standing just like they always have been; but the white pieces are standing on worse squares'!

He finishes up with a fantastic study. I'd never seen it before, but I'll never forget it! White to mate in 8 moves! The crux of the solution is to reach the same position as now but with

Black's right to castling removed! I can't believe it hangs together!

Nikola Petrovic
Nenad 1959

1.♕b7 ♖d8 2.♕b3 ♖a8 3.♗d3 ♖h1+ 4.♗b1 ♖h8 5.♕c3 ♖h7 6.♕f6 f2 7.♘xh7 f1♕ 8.♕f8 Mate. Amazing!

All in all, another fantastic book from Quality Chess!

■ ■ ■

Emmanuel Bricard, a French Grandmaster and trainer, is a name familiar to me from my professional days. I remember him as a creative and very tricky player, so you can imagine my confusion at seeing *Strategic Chess Exercises* (New In Chess). I would not have imagined that he would ever have written a book on this theme! Once again, I have been pleasantly surprised! It's not at all easy to put together an exercise book for strategic problems. Unlike tactical problems – where there should be a proven solution to each puzzle – (poorly chosen) strategic puzzles can easily lead to the reader thinking 'well that's your opinion'! Bricard has managed to put together a high-quality set of exercises that mimics quite well the decision-making process you go through during a game. Just like in a game, there is both

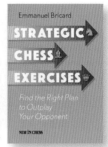

Strategic Chess Exercises by Emmanuel Bricard
New In Chess, 2018
★★★★★

a creativity challenge (finding a good idea) and an implementation challenge (working your way through the plusses and minuses of the various ways of executing your idea and choosing the best one on balance). I have had no qualms in recommending this book already to students looking to improve their game, and I also made grateful use of it in my own preparations for one of my infrequent playing appearances at the 4NCL in May. Bricard's explanations of each puzzle are extremely clear and detailed and through clever layout, it's quite possible to look at the solution of one puzzle without necessarily seeing the solution of the next puzzle.

Bricard's frame of reference is fairly broad. Quite naturally, Vassily Smyslov scores the best with nine examples, but it's good to see many examples from lesser-known players such as Amos Burn (three examples) and Jan Smejkal (five examples).

Let's take a look at one of Smejkal's games (a wonderful player by the way – has there ever been a Best Games Collection of his?). One of my own games that I was most pleased about since I started playing chess again is a game against Ostmø from the Oslo Open in 2011 where I won a pretty tame-looking opposite-coloured bishop position with good play, and especially with excellent reasoning. I felt that I'd understood the subtleties of the position very well and managed to make something out of absolutely nothing. If I'd known this game of Smejkal's played in 1974, I probably would have needed to think a bit less! It's a great template for playing this type of simple position:

'Markos has a host of original ideas and a wonderfully witty and enthusiastic way of bringing them across.'

Klaus Uwe Müller
Jan Smejkal
Halle 1974

position after 14.♖xe4

White has the most active bishop and a space advantage. He has good chances of taking the initiative, if Black plays passively, by advancing his h-pawn after having completed his development. The c3- and d4-pawns control the centre and limit the action of the f6-bishop, but they are sort of blocked because the advance of either one would weaken the dark squares and hinder the movement of the white bishop.

14...b5 Black's plan is to put pressure on the dark squares by playing ...b5-b4 at the right time, followed by an exchange on c3 and ...c7-c5, and this will create a weak pawn and weak squares in the White position. It's an attempt to sharpen the play. **15.♗b3 a5 16.a3 b4 17.♕e2 bxc3 18.bxc3 ♖ab8 19.♗c4 c5 20.h4 cxd4 21.cxd4 ♖b6**

A multi-purpose move that allows play on the b- or d-files (by ...♖f8-b8 or ...♖b6-d6) and may prepare ...e7-e6. **22.♖e1 ♗xd4** 22...e6 was a still better move according to Bricard, when after 23.♕d2 ♖d8 24.♕xa5 ♗xd4,

The Modernized Reti
by Adrien Demuth
Thinkers Publishing,
2017
★★★★☆

Black has a clear advantage because of the better security of his king. **23.♖xe7 ♕f5 24.g4 ♕f6 25.g5 ♕f5 26.♖d1 ♖b2 27.♖xd4 ♖xe2 28.♗xe2 ♕c5 29.♖dd7 ♕xa3 30.♔g2 ♕b4 31.♔g3 a4 32.♗f3 ♕b8+ 33.♔g2 a3 34.♗d5 ♕f4 35.♖e4 ♕f5 36.♖d6 a2 37.♖a4 ♕e5** 0-1.

In conclusion, highly recommended: I'm afraid I have to give this one 5 stars too!

■ ■ ■

It's really more than time for me to find some bad books to be nasty about this month, but this has proved to be too tough an undertaking. I recently received *The Modernized Reti* (Thinkers Publishing) by another French grandmaster, Adrien Demuth. The blurb at the back states that he learnt his chess at the age of 7 in Tahiti, which is one of the more exotic locations I've heard of! I wonder if anyone can beat that? The book covers a repertory based around 1.♘f3 and 2.c4 in which the fianchetto of the king's bishop (with g3 and ♗g2) plays a major role. The big problem with writing a book on the Réti is the choice that Black has early on, and thus the number of transpositions that White must be aware of when building up his repertory. Although I do rather miss an overall index of the variations chosen for the book, Demuth does a good and thorough job of dealing with all the possibilities. There is also a lot of original analysis and ideas. I'm not an expert on all the Black systems, but looking at the anti-Queen's Gambit Accepted and anti-Tarrasch sections, I was impressed by the work that the author had put in. The one dampener on the whole thing is the rather mysterious cover. There's a chessboard, a knight, and some multi-coloured pawns, one

Playing 1.e4 e5
A Classical Repertoire
by Nikolaos Ntirlis
Quality Chess, 2016
★★★★☆

of which is facing downwards. I have no idea whatsoever what it's supposed to signify! Apart from that, an excellent book recommended for any player burning to play the Réti!

■ ■ ■

We'll finish off this month's review with an opening book that stayed in my bookcase for far too long, and that definitely deserves to be mentioned: *Playing 1.e4 e5 – A Classical Repertoire* by Nikolas Ntirlis (Quality Chess). Taking the Breyer System:

1.e4 e5 2.♘f3 ♘c6 3.♗b5 a6 4.♗a4 ♘f6 5.0-0 ♗e7 6.♖e1 b5 7.♗b3 d6 8.c3 0-0 9.h3 ♘b8

as the basis for a 1.e4 e5 repertoire, Ntirlis provides a complete repertoire for Black, dealing with all White sidelines (and there are many!). I was particularly impressed by the effort Ntirlis has put in to find solutions against lines such as the Vienna or the Bishop's Opening that do not demand too much memorization. It's probably pretty much the ideal repertoire for a player wanting to take up 1.e4 e5 without having to learn the whole world! Apart from that, Ntirlis does his normal thorough, creative job. What can I say more, it's a really good one-volume book for learning 1.e4 e5 ! ■

Hans Ree

Going for Karpov's head

Genna Sosonko's latest book *Evil-Doer* is a 'warts and all' memoir about Viktor Kortchnoi. Like his previous book about David Bronstein, it is published by Elk and Ruby, a new firm with a small but interesting list of publications. **HANS REE** found *Evil-Doer* Sosonko's most personal book; writing about Kortchnoi, he gives the outline of a self-portrait.

Kortchnoi's photograph on the cover of the book seemed familiar to me. I may have seen it before, but I am not sure, because his characteristic expression can be seen on many photos: crooked smile, twinkling eyes. We see genuine enjoyment, tinged with some malice, as if he is telling a hilarious story about an opponent he has beaten.

As Genna explains, 'Evil-Doer' was a term used by Soviet players after Viktor's defection from the Soviet Union in 1976, but Genna is well aware that the defector, always ready for battle, would have appreciated the term himself. 'How do you want to be remembered after your death?', a journalist asked him once. I want them to say that I was no angel, said Viktor.

I think I will be excused for using the informal 'Genna' now and then instead of his full name. I have known Genna for the biggest part of my life, and we live near each other and frequent the same supermarket. About halfway between our homes, Jan Timman used to live above a chocolate shop that bears the proud name of House of Van Wely. In the past, the three of us had lived quite near each other in a different part of Amsterdam, where the geographical midpoint of our abodes was the artists' club De Kring, where many chess players used to meet. It was a small world. Alas, Timman has moved to the city of Arnhem many years ago.

I will also occasionally use the informal 'Viktor', although with some hesitation. But in 1977, when I was one of his seconds for his Candidates match against Petrosian, we shared a bed one night in a hotel in Switzerland, and I think that gives me the right to informality.

The subtitle of Genna's book is 'Half a Century with Viktor Korchnoi'. Indeed, no one seems more qualified to write a biographical memoir of Kortchnoi than Genna, not only because he is a fine writer, but also because there is probably no one in chess who knew Viktor better than he did, all the way from their years in the Soviet Union to Kortchnoi's final days in Switzerland, where he died in 2016 at the age of 85.

A precarious relationship

Genna emigrated from the Soviet Union in 1972; Kortchnoi defected in 1976. They used to live quite near each other in Leningrad, although not in the same street. By the way, chess coach Gennady Nesis has written that he lived opposite our Gennady Sosonko in the same Leningrad street, Baskov periulok, and that a certain Vladimir Putin, who would become very well-known to the world, also lived in that street for quite some time. Putin cannot have had much contact with the future grandmasters in his street. He was too young.

In the Soviet Union, Sosonko didn't have a great career as a player, but he was recognized as a man with a great insight, someone who could, at a glance, discern the essential elements of a position and the probable outcome of the struggle. He was a coach of Mikhail Tal and of Kortchnoi, and assisted the latter in his Candidates match against Petrosian in 1971.

After Sosonko had left the Soviet Union they met again at the tournament in Hastings of 1975/76, and when Kortchnoi himself had defected after the 1976 IBM tournament in Amsterdam, their relationship was resumed with ups and downs.

Sosonko had lost that game in Hastings and was irritated with Kortchnoi for several reasons. When Kortchnoi knocked on his door the next evening, he invited him in and started holding forth. Genna writes: 'I was hot-headed, young (younger than I thought, in fact), and here was a chance to point out everything: his engrained Soviet, Communist Party mentality (despite all his anecdotes and mockery of the system), his opportunism, our conversation with Lavrov [a Soviet professor, as far as I can make out not related to the present foreign minister – H.R], and even his slavish dependence on chess.' Kortchnoi heard him out and said: 'Have you finished?' Genna had not finished. He repeated his reproaches in even stronger terms, and while he talked it seemed clear to him that their relation had broken down, probably forever.

Kortchnoi reacted unexpectedly calmly and said: 'You know, Gennady Borisovich, maybe everything you say is true. Maybe. But you also play chess as a form of self-expression, and some of your personality traits may also be unpleasant. You're no angel yourself. Believe me – no angel. Well, accept me with all my defects, just as I accept you with yours.'

Genna was stunned and disarmed by this reaction, which was quite out of character for Kortchnoi. He mumbled some conciliatory words and they set off for dinner together.

With knife and orange

In an introductory chapter, Genna writes that he considers it his duty to write everything he knows about Kortchnoi and to give a portrait, 'warts and all'. The warts are the counterparts of the qualities for which Kortchnoi is admired: his total dedication to chess, at the cost of everything else; his egocentricity and his often aggressive honesty. He thrived on conflict, it often seemed.

His defection had been a bombshell not only in the Soviet chess world, where it became a matter of grave concern to the highest Party echelons. In 1978, he played against Karpov for the World Championship in Baguio, in the Philippines. For the Soviet delegation he was the traitor, the enemy of the great Soviet state that incorporated the ambitions of every honest worker in the world.

Later he would recall to Genna: 'Oh, it was an unforgettable feeling. You walk past a line of hate-filled eyes and each person in this line wants to cut you into little pieces. You haven't lived until you have experienced this.'

Of course, Viktor contributed his fair share of animosity. Genna quotes the Swiss lawyer Alban Brodbeck, who was part of Viktor's team from 1978 to 1981 and who described an amazing scene. In Baguio in 1978, Viktor was assisted by an American couple who were members of the Indian Ananda Marga sect and were apparently wanted in India on the suspicion of stabbing a diplomat. In Baguio they went under the names Dada and Didi.

Brodbeck said: 'Once, I entered his suite, not expecting strangers there, and came across an astounding spectacle. Korchnoi, dressed in an eastern outfit, was performing a ritual dance. He held a knife in one hand and an orange in the other, which, they told me, represented Karpov's head.' According to Didi, this was done so that Viktor could accumulate cosmic energy.

From outcast to guest of honour

At that time, he felt as if he was struggling alone against the biggest country in the world. His greatest enemies were Petrosian, Karpov and Baturinsky, the chief of the Soviet delegation in Baguio and the head of Soviet chess.

But times changed. The Soviet Union and the Party system collapsed and everything became different. Genna writes that when Baturinsky, the dark colonel, as Viktor had called him, died in 2002, Kortchnoi felt as if a piece of himself had been torn off. I can understand this. At a certain age you become thankful even to your enemies for the fact that they are still alive to assure you that the old days are not yet completely buried.

After the collapse of the Soviet Union, Viktor became a guest of honour in Russia and in all the newly independent states. He accepted an invitation for a Petrosian Memorial tournament and played alongside Karpov in the Russian team competition for the Southern Ural's team from Chelyabinsk.

Who needs legs?

He always wanted to play, even in his final years after a stroke had taken away his strength. Condemned to a wheelchair, he said to Genna: 'What does a chess player needs legs for?'

I had the privilege to be one of Viktor's seconds during two of his Candidates matches: against Tigran

'He surely knows that the great Viktor Kortchnoi in his chess heaven would roar with approving laughter when reading this beautiful book.'

Petrosian in 1977 and against Lajos Portisch in 1983. I am not sure if I was of great help, but at least I don't have to feel guilty, since he won both matches.

I remember his humour, his boisterous laugh, and above all his untiring dedication to chess, which was truly inspiring. 'To the end' was a frequent expression of his, meaning that analysis should never be vague and that chess problems are there to be solved precisely.

Genna has portrayed him with sternness and also, I think, with love, 'warts and all'. He surely knows that the great Viktor Kortchnoi in his chess heaven, perhaps while studying a little line in the French to surprise the ghost of Geza Maroczy in a return match, would roar with approving laughter when reading this beautiful book: 'Did I ever pretend to be an angel?' ∎

Jan Timman

Baden-Baden anyway

The joint final rounds of the Bundesliga in Berlin were not enough to decide on the 2017/18 champions, as top-favourites Baden-Baden and their closest rivals Solingen finished with equal match points. **JAN TIMMAN** looks at the exciting finish of the most professional club competition in the world.

O nce again Berlin was the German capital of chess. Slightly over a month after an unforgettable Candidates tournament had ended in a victory for Fabiano Caruana, the final three rounds of the Bundesliga took place there – for the third consecutive year. In a spacious room of the Maritim Hotel, 16 eight-player teams were going to battle it out. The first 12 rounds had taken place elsewhere, in various places around the country. The three final rounds were exciting, because both Baden-Baden and Solingen were leading with the same number of match points.

The Baden-Baden team has been incredibly strong for years. In the '70s and '80s, there were matches between the Soviet Union and the Rest of the World. You couldn't imagine stronger teams than those. But Baden-Baden can draw on top players from the entire world, which makes it stronger than any other team. Not that it prevented Solingen from reclaiming the title two years ago – for the 12th time! – and from being dangerous rivals again this season. Solingen's secret rests mainly in the homogeneity of its team. Besides the top players Pentala Harikrishna, Richard Rapport and Markus Ragger, they can draw on a contingent of Dutch grandmasters that are good friends with one another.

In the first six rounds of the competition, neither Baden-Baden nor Solingen put a foot wrong. Baden-Baden usually made the better scores, but that was of minor importance. In the Bundesliga, the most important thing is match points. In Round 7, Solingen got no more

than a draw against Bremen, and in the next round, Baden-Baden suffered the same fate against SK Hamburg. In Round 10, the two top clubs played each other, with Harikrishna-Vachier-Lagrave at the first board. All games but one were drawn: Erwin l'Ami clinched the match for Solingen by defeating Arkadij Naiditsch in an excellent game.

Erwin l'Ami
Arkadij Naiditsch
Aachen 2018 (10)
Queen's Gambit Declined,
Cambridge Springs Variation

1.d4 ♘f6 2.c4 e6 3.♘f3 d5 4.♘c3 ♘bd7 5.♗g5 c6 6.e3 ♕a5 7.♘d2

The most solid system against the Cambridge Springs.
7...dxc4 8.♗xf6 ♘xf6 9.♘xc4 ♕c7 10.♖c1 ♗e7 11.g3 0-0 12.♗g2

♖d8 13.0-0 ♘d5 14.a3 ♗d7 15.b4

A strategically important move. White is going to exert pressure on the queenside.
15...♗e8 16.♕b3 ♖ac8 17.♘e5
This knight move allows Black to free himself. More accurate was 17.♘e2, intending to continue manoeuvring. I was successful with this approach in a game against Hort, Amsterdam 1980.

The old and new champions of Baden-Baden: Sven Noppes (team captain), Wolfgang Grenke (sponsor), Rustam Kasimdzhanov, Vishy Anand, Patrick Bittner (club president), Radek Wojtaszek, Mickey Adams, Maxime Vachier-Lagrave, Fabiano Caruana and Etienne Bacrot.

A second piece materializes on this vital square.

29...♖b7 30.♖1c4 Stronger was 30.♘db2, intending to take the knight to c4.

30...♘g6 31.♘f4 ♘xf4 32.gxf4 ♕d8 A better defence was 32...♖f8, e.g. 33.♕f3 ♗b4 34.f5 g6, and White won't find it easy to make progress.

33.♕f3 ♖b8 34.f5

17...♕b8

With 17...a5! Black could have shaken off the white pressure. After 18.bxa5 ♕xa5 19.♘xd5 cxd5 White has no advantage.

18.♘d3 ♖c7 19.♖c2 ♖dc8 20.♖fc1 ♘f6 21.a4 b6 22.b5

Good timing. The queenside structure is fixed to White's advantage.

22...cxb5

22...c5 would have run into the solid 23.♘e5. After 23...cxd4 24.exd4 ♖d8 25.♖d1 White retains serious pressure.

23.axb5 ♘d7 24.♗c6!

Systematic and strong. White is

gaining more and more territory on the queenside.

24...a5

25.e4 25.d5 e5 26.♘e4 ♖a7 27.♖c4 was strong, but the text is more thematic. White wants to advance his e-pawn to e5 in order to restrict Black's counterplay even further.

25...♖d8 26.e5 ♖a7

More tenacious was 26...♘f8. White cements his advantage with 27.d5 exd5 28.♘xd5 ♗xc6 29.bxc6 ♘e6, and now 30.♕a2! is the most accurate move. He is in no rush to take on c7.

27.♘a4 ♘f8 28.♗xe8 ♖xe8 29.♖c6

34...exf5 Conceding too much territory. More tenacious was 34...♗f8.

35.♕xf5 ♗b4 36.♖c7 ♖f8

37.♖d7 Devastating. **37...g6** After 37...♕h4, 38.♖cc7 would have been winning. **38.♖xd8 gxf5 39.♖xb8 ♖xb8 40.♔g2** The technical stage is easy. **40...♔f8 41.♔f3 f6 42.♔f4 fxe5+ 43.dxe5 ♖d8 44.♘xb6 ♖d2**

'Baden-Baden can draw on top players from the entire world, which makes it stronger than any other team.'

45.♔xf5 ♖xf2+ 46.♔e6

Black resigned.

It was the second time this season that l'Ami was the match winner for Solingen. In the second round against Bayern Munich, he had also been the only player that won his game.

After 11 rounds, Solingen was leading by two match points and looked certain to win the title, but they lost to Hockenheim in Round 12, which made for a tense finale in Berlin. Both clubs had come to the German capital at full capacity, and neither made a mistake: both teams won all their three matches. It was good to see that Aronian (Baden-Baden), after his catastrophic performance in the Candidates, gave a good account of himself in Berlin.

Levon Aronian
Mykhaylo Oleksiyenko
Berlin 2018 (14)
Queen's Gambit Declined

1.d4 d5 2.c4 e6 3.♘f3 ♘f6 4.♘c3 a6 5.cxd5 exd5 6.♗g5 ♗e6 7.e3 ♘bd7 8.♗d3 ♗d6

This system has been played a lot in the last two years. Carlsen has tried it out as well, but only in rapid games.

9.♗f4 This is not new in itself, but it is usually played later. Remarkably enough, Aronian also played this against Carlsen during the World Rapid Championship. That game was quickly drawn, because it wasn't important to either of them. Carlsen had already won the title.

9...♕e7 10.0-0 0-0 11.h3 c6 12.♕c2 ♖fe8 13.♖ae1 g6 14.♗g5

Afterwards, Aronian said in a short interview for the Bundesliga website: 'Generally you start to understand this system when you play it, since the computer is not very good at it.' At first sight, the text seems to make no sense, but it is well thought out nevertheless. Now that Black has advanced his g-pawn, it will not be easy to chase the bishop from g5.

14...♕f8 The best continuation. 14...♔g7 would have been met strongly by 15.e4. After 15...dxe4 16.♘xe4 h6 17.♘xd6 ♕xd6 18.♗c1!, White has excellent attacking chances. He is threatening to take his queen to d2.

15.a3 Play on both wings.

15...♖ac8 16.b4 b5

This advance is not bad in itself, but grandmasters from previous generations would probably never have played it. In *Timman's Titans*, I feature the game Benko-Petrosian, in which Black decides to advance his b-pawn in the certainty that he will get an initiative on the queenside. This is not the case here. But due to tactical factors, the text turns out to be just about playable.

> **'It was good to see that Aronian, after his catastrophic performance in the Candidates, gave a good account of himself in Berlin.'**

A good alternative was 16...♘h5. After 17.e4 f6 18.♗d2 ♘f4! Black has sufficient counterplay.

17.♘d2 On its way to b3. White could also have played his other knight: 17.♘e2, but to no advantage. After 17...♘h5 18.♘f4 h6! 19.♘xe6 ♖xe6 20.♗h4 ♘b6, Black controls the queenside, with the white bishop pair making little or no difference.

17...♘h5 18.♘b3 h6 19.♗h4 g5 20.♕d1

20...♘g7 Too passive. Black should have kept up the pressure on the kingside with 20...♘df6, after which White has the following possibilities:

ANALYSIS DIAGRAM

A) 21.♗g3 ♗xg3 (more accurate than 21...♘xg3 22.fxg3 ♘d7 when after 23.♔h2

♕g7 24.e4 White is slightly better) 22.fxg3 g4 23.♘c5 ♕g7 24.h4 ♘xg3 25.♖f4 ♘gh5 26.♖ff1, with equal play.

B) 21.♗e2 gxh4 22.♗xh5 ♕g7 23.♔h1 ♘xh5 24.♕xh5 ♕g6 25.♕d1 (not 25.♕xh4 in view of 25...♕c2) 25...♔h7, and here, too, the chances are equal;

21.♗g3 f5 22.♗xd6 ♕xd6

23.♘c5 The thematic move to restrict Black's counterplay. 23.♕c2 would have allowed Black to go 23...f4.

23...♘xc5 24.dxc5 ♕e5 25.♘e2 ♗d7

Black persists in his passivity. After 25...f4 26.♘d4 ♕f6 27.♗b1, White would get a winning advantage. Opening the position would suit White.

26.♘d4 ♖e7 27.a4 ♖ce8 28.♗c2 h5 29.axb5 axb5 30.♕d3 g4

31.hxg4 Maybe it was inaccurate to open the h-file. After 31.♖a1 gxh3 32.gxh3 ♕f6 33.♖a7, White would clearly be better. Black can play 33...♘e6 in an attempt to grab the initiative with a pawn sacrifice, but White retains control with 34.♘xf5 ♖f7 35.♕d1.

31...hxg4 32.g3

32...♖a8

Obvious; yet the rook has no business on the queenside at all, because White will take control of the a-file. Here, too, Black should have sacrificed a pawn for counterplay. After 32...♘e6! 33.♘xf5 ♖h7 34.♘h4 ♘g5 35.♔g2 ♖f7, Black has some compensation for the pawn.

33.♖a1 ♖ee8 34.♕c3 ♕e7 35.♔g2 ♔f7 36.♖h1 Thematic. The white rooks are put on the open files.

36...♕f6 37.♖h7

37...♖xa1 Black has a choice between biting the dust on the a-file or doing so on the h-file. 37...♖h8 38.♖xh8 ♖xh8 39.♖a7 was equally hopeless.

38.♕xa1 ♔g8 39.♕h1 Devastating doubling. **39...♕g5 40.♖h6** Black resigned.

Play-off match

If two teams finish on top with the same number of match points, the Bundesliga regulations stipulate a face-off between the two. The last time this had happened was 13 years ago, when Werder Bremen beat SG Porz. The teams weren't so strong then.

Baden-Baden had the highest number of board points, which entitled them to hosting the play-off.

It was difficult to find a suitable date. Other events had been planned for the weekends, and the players' commitments obviously also had to be taken into account. In the end, they settled on May 24th, three days before the start of Norway Chess. This would enable Baden-Baden's three top boards (Fabiano Caruana, Maxime Vachier-Lagrave and Vishy Anand) to fit the match into their schedules. Solingen managed to line up Anish Giri, who had not played in the regular competition. But they had little luck otherwise. Pentala Harikrishna was playing in the Chinese league, and Richard Rapport had commitments in Hungary.

But the club suffered another, far more serious blow: four days before the decider, Herbert Scheidt died at the age of 73. For several decades, Scheidt had been the driving force behind the club, and had regularly sponsored its activities.

The match was played in the Kristallsaal of the Kulturhaus LA8, a 19th-century palace renovated by sponsor Grenke. A striking detail was that there wasn't a single German player in the line-ups (Naiditsch is playing for Azerbaijan these days). The match never got really exciting. Solingen was suffering on many boards. The first blow was dealt on Board 4.

Peter Svidler
Jan Smeets
Baden-Baden 2018 (1)

position after 20...♘g6

After a Petroff Defence, White has managed to create a slight advantage. Now Svidler (Baden-Baden) takes a remarkable decision.

21.f4 White expands his kingside ter-

On Board 1, Anish Giri saved Solingen's honour by beating Fabiano Caruana from a virtually equal position, but Baden-Baden's victory was never in any doubt.

ritory. The drawback is that he provides the black bishop with an open diagonal, but Black has too little space to exploit it. **21...♕f6 22.g3 ♖ad8 23.♖e3 ♘f8 24.♖de1 ♕d6 25.f5 f6**

26.♘xc6 Smeets was already in serious time-trouble here. All the more reason to play the alternative 26.♘c4, intending to meet 26...♕d7 with 27.♕f2. But Svidler is aiming for an endgame in which Black will be forced to play very accurately. **26...♕xc6 27.♗b4 ♖xe3 28.♖xe3 ♕xc2 29.♗xc2 b6 30.♖e7 ♘d7 31.♗a4**

31...c5? After this panicky pawn push

White gets a large advantage. Correct was 31...c6. After 32.♔f2 a5 33.♗d6 ♘f8! 34.♗c7 ♖d7 the black defences remain intact. **32.♗e1!** The best square for the bishop.

32...♘b8 Initially, Black had probably pinned his hopes on 32...b5, but after 33.♗a5 ♖c8 34.♖xd7 ♘c6 35.♗b3+ c4 36.♗xc4+ bxc4 37.♖d6, White would have a winning advantage. **33.dxc5 b5 34.♗d1 ♘c6 35.♖c7 ♘d4**

It looks as if Black has created some activity, but it is not enough. **36.♗a5 ♘xf5 37.♖xg7+** The sim-

plest way to the win. **37...♔xg7 38.♗xd8 ♘e3 39.♗h5 ♗c6** More tenacious was 39...♘c4, when White must play 40.♗e8 ♔f8 41.♗d7 ♔f7 42.c6 to convert his advantage. **40.♗a5 ♘c4 41.♗c3**

Dominating the knight. **41...a5 42.♔f2 b4 43.axb4 axb4 44.♗xb4 ♘xb2 45.♗e2 ♗a4 46.♔e1** And now the knight will be lost. Black resigned.

Not long afterwards, Predrag Nikolic (Solingen) quietly succumbed to Rustam Kasimdzhanov. Baden-Baden seemed to be on course for a resounding victory, but then Giri (Solingen) managed to outplay Caruana from a virtually equal position.

Anish Giri
Fabiano Caruana
Baden-Baden 2018 (1)
Petroff Defence, Marshall Variation

1.e4 e5 2.♘f3 ♘f6 3.♘xe5 d6 4.♘f3 ♘xe4 5.d4 d5 6.♗d3 ♗d6 7.0-0 0-0 8.c4 c6 9.♘c3 ♘xc3 10.bxc3 dxc4 11.♗xc4 ♗f5 12.♗g5

With this bishop move, Nepomniachtchi scored a spectacular win over Li Chao last year.

12...♛a5 The best queen move. It had been played in Cornette-Tregubov, France 2018, two weeks earlier. The alternative 12...♜c7 yields White a strong initiative. In Nepomniachtchi-Li Chao, Sharjah 2017, there followed: 13.♜e1 h6 14.♘h4 ♗h7 15.♗xh6! ♗xh2+ 16.♔h1 ♗f4 17.♗xg7! ♔xg7 18.♛g4+, and White had a decisive attack.

13.♘h4 ♗e6 14.♗xe6 ♛xg5 15.♘f3

15...♛d8 Caruana took a long time to decide on this retreat. Tregubov had played 15...♛a5. Both queen moves seem to be playable.

16.♗b3 ♘d7 17.♜e1

White is slightly better, mainly because his bishop is slightly stronger than its black counterpart.

17...g6 18.g3 ♔g7 19.♛d3 ♘f6 20.♜ad1 ♜c8 21.h4 ♜c7 22.♔g2

♜e7 23.♜xe7 ♛xe7 24.♜e1 ♛d7

25.♘e5 Unable to find another way to increase the pressure, Giri decides to swap his knight for the black bishop. The computer is not impressed, but in practice, the resulting position is not easy to defend for Black.

25...♗xe5 26.♜xe5 ♜e8 27.♛e2

27...h5 Fixing the position in this way sometimes leads to problems for Black

in the endgame, but for the moment he has nothing to worry about. And White was definitely threatening to advance his h-pawn. After, for example, 27...a5 28.h5, White would be in the driver's seat.

28.f3 White's plan is clear: he wants to launch an offensive on the kingside by advancing his g-pawn. But this is not going to happen for a while.

28...♔f8 29.♜xe8+

29...♘xe8

There was nothing against 29...♛xe8, because in this situation, Black need not fear the bishop vs knight ending. After 30.♛d2 ♔g7, he won't need to worry either.

30.♛e5 Now White has a firm grip on his initiative. The white queen will be hard to chase out of its dominant position.

30...♘d6

31.♔f2 A venomous little move that packs a hidden threat.

31...♔g8

An understandable move in itself: the prospect of a check on h8 is slightly disturbing. Yet 31...♛d8 was the correct move, stopping the advance of the white g-pawn.

32.g4!

White launches his offensive.

32...hxg4 33.fxg4 ♛d8 34.♔f3 ♔h7 35.h5 f6 36.♛e6

Black has managed to chase the queen from e5, but it has found a new dominant position. Black's situation is critical.

36...♔g7 37.♔f4 a5 38.a3

The natural reaction, but 38.a4, to restrict Black's counterplay, would have been more accurate.

38...gxh5

There was no more time for half measures. Black should have sacrificed a pawn with 38...a4!, when White has two possible reactions:

ANALYSIS DIAGRAM

A) 39.♗xa4 ♘f7 40.♗c2 ♘g5, and the knight has an excellent position. Black has some compensation for the pawn;

B) 39.♗a2 gxh5 40.gxh5 ♔h6 (40...♛f8 is also possible) 41.♗b1 ♘b5 42.♛f7 ♛c7+, and the bishop-knight ending is tenable.

39.gxh5 ♔h6 40.♗c2

Indirectly protecting the h-pawn, and mobilizing his bishop.

40...♛f8

Black persists in his passive defence, and this will soon lead to his downfall. His best practical chance was 40...♘b5, after which White needs to play some accurate moves to win. After 41.♔g4! ♘xa3 42.♗d3 ♛f8 43.♔f3! his attack would strike home, e.g. 43...a4 44.♛e3+ ♔g7 45.♛g1+ ♔h8 46.♛g6 ♛g7 47.♛e8+ ♛g8 48.♛e7 ♘b5 49.h6, and mate will follow soon.

41.♔f3 ♘e8 42.♔g2 ♘d6

43.♔f2

All White needs to do is play tempo moves. Black is completely defenceless.

43...b6 44.♔f3 ♘e8

Or 44...c5 45.♛g4, and wins.

45.♛xc6 ♘d6 46.♛xb6 ♛e7 47.♛b8 ♘f7 48.♛g8 ♘g5+ 49.♔f4 ♘h3+ 50.♔f5 ♛d7+ 51.♔xf6 Black resigned.

Giri had at least saved Solingen's honour. That's what they had to settle for. Markus Ragger and Mads Andersen managed to scrape a draw against Maxime Vachier-Lagrave and Etienne Bacrot, and the hero of the previous match, Erwin l'Ami, could also call himself lucky with his draw against Radoslaw Wojtaszek.

And so Baden-Baden won their 12th national championship, equalling Solingen's record. ■

Germany Bundesliga 2017/18		
	MP	BP
1 OSG Baden-Baden	27	86.5
2 SG Solingen	27	84.5
3 SV 1930 Hockenheim	22	76
4 SV Werder Bremen	22	74.5
5 Schachfreunde Deizisau	18	67.5
6 USV TU Dresden	18	62
7 DJK Aufwärts Aachen	16	62.5
8 SK Schwäbisch Hall	16	61.5
9 SF Berlin 1903	15	57.5
10 Hamburger SK	12	63
11 SV Mülheim Nord	11	52.5
12 SV 1920 Hofheim	11	48
13 MSA Zugzwang 82	8	44
14 SG Speyer-Schwegenheim	8	42.5
15 FC Bayern München	6	45.5
16 SK Norderstedt 1975	3	32
Baden-Baden beats Solingen		
4½-3½ in play-off match		

1. Shuvalova-M.Muzychuk
Vysoke Tatry 2018

25.♖xb7+! ♔c8 Both captures lose the queen: 25...♘xb7 26.♕xe6 or 25...♔xb7 26.♘c5+. **26.♕xe6+ ♘xe6 27.♖xe7** winning a piece.

2. Xiong-Robson
St. Louis 2018

37...♖xg2+! White resigned since after 37...♖xg2+ 38.♔xg2 ♕g4+ king moves lead to mate whereas 39.♘g3 ♕xe6 loses the queen.

3. Shevchenko-Mutschnik
Bundesliga 2017

40.♖f3! ♕xf3 40...♕g7 41.♗h6. **41.♕h8+ ♔e7 42.♗g5+** Black resigned in view of 42...♔f6 (42...♔d7 43.♕d8 mate) 43.♕g7+ ♔e8 44.♗xf6.

4. Van Wely-Hausrath
Belgium tt 2018

Black's diagonals are insufficiently protected: **34.♘xe6! ♕xe6** Equally hopeless is 34...♖xd1 35.♕c3+ ♖d4 36.♘xf8. **35.♖xd5 ♕xd5 36.♕c3+ ♔g8 37.♗c4** And Black resigned shortly after.

5. Williams-A.l'Ami
St Clement Bay 2018

52...♕e1+! 53.♖xe1 On 53.♗f1 ♗d5+ 54.♖g2, 54...♕xd1 55.♕xd1 ♘f2+ is elegant and crushing. **53...♖xe1+ 54.♗f1 ♖xf1+** White threw in the towel as 55.♔g2 ♘e1+! protects Black's rook at the same time.

6. Bauer-Colmenares
Zurich 2018

21.♗g6! Black resigned. After 21...fxg6 22.♘xg6 or 21...♖f8 22.♗xf7+ ♖xf7 23.♘g6 his queen is caught; 21...0-0 22.♘xd5 ♘xd5 23.♗xf7+ ♖xf7 24.♕h7+ is checkmate and 21...♗xf4 22.♗xf7+ ♔f8 23.exf4 is cheerless.

7. Balog-Van Dooren
Bundesliga 2017

17.♗g5! ♕xg5 18.e7+ cxd5 After 18...♗e6 19.exf8♕+ ♖xf8 White can choose between the simple 20.♗xe6+ ♘xe6 21.♖xd6 and the flashy 20.♖xb7!. Now the flamboyant way is the only way: **19.♕h8+!** And Black resigned.

8. Saric-Bosiocic
Croatia 2018

41.♖hg1 Dislodging the rook from the back rank. **41...♖h7** 41...♖g8 42.h6. **42.bxa6! ♖xb1 43.a7** The pawn is unstoppable... **43...♘c6 44.a8♕ ♖b8 45.♕a6...** and the newborn queen has an escape square. **45...♖b2 46.♖c1** Black resigned.

9. Boruchovsky-Kozak
Budapest 2018

37.♖d8! ♔g6? 38.♖h8 Black resigned in view of 38...♘b6 39.♖xa8 ♘xa8 40.♕d7. After 37...♗xd8 White would have had to find 38.♕d5+! ♔g6 39.♕g8! ♘d6 40.h4!! (opening the c1-h6 diagonal) 40...gxh4 41.♗d7! h3+ 42.♔h2 and wins.

Bassem Amin

CURRENT ELO: 2679

DATE OF BIRTH: September 9, 1988

PLACE OF BIRTH: Tanta, Egypt

PLACE OF RESIDENCE: Tanta, Egypt

What is your favourite city?
Dubai.

What was the last great meal you had?
I love pizza, and especially Pizza Hut.

What drink brings a smile to your face?
Milkshake caramel.

Which book would you give to a dear friend?
The Five Love Languages by Gary Chapman.

What book is currently on your bedside table?
The Holy Bible.

What is your all-time favourite movie?
The Dark Knight and *The Dark Knight Rises*. I like super-hero movies.

What music are you currently listening to?
All of Me, John Legend.

Who is your favourite chess player?
Garry Kasparov. A great player, a unique personality, the best player in the world for such a long time!

Is there a chess book that had a profound influence on you?
I am not a big book reader, I mainly work on the computer.

What was your best result ever?
In 2017, I won both Lake Sevan and the Abu Dhabi Masters.

And the best game you played?
My win against GM Vera Gonzalez, Cappelle-la-Grande 2012.

What was the most exciting chess game you have ever seen?
Kasparov-Topalov, Wijk aan Zee 2001.

What is your favourite square?
As I am a King's Indian Attack player: d3.

Do chess players have typical shortcomings?
Sometimes laziness!

What are chess players particularly good at (except for chess)?
Organized thinking.

Do you have any superstitions concerning chess?
I try not to have any. When I lose wearing a certain shirt, I try to wear it again and win!

Who do you follow on Twitter?
Chess players and chess media, some football and sports news. Egyptian politicians, actors...

Where is your favourite place in the world?
Home!

When were you happiest?
Many great moments in many tournaments. In personal life: my wedding day, becoming a father, holding my baby every day is great. ☺

Who or what would you like to be if you weren't yourself?
Maybe a footballer like Mo Salah!

Which three people would you like to invite for dinner?
Mo Salah, Garry Kasparov and Pope Tawadros.

How do you relax?
During a tournament I watch movies.

What is your life motto?
The best is yet to come!

What is the best piece of advice you have ever been given?
The more you sweat in training, the less you bleed in battle.

Is there something you'd love to learn?
Languages, especially Russian, French, Dutch.

What is your greatest fear?
The most important thing for me is to make my family happy and proud, and as long as they are, I have no fears.

And your greatest regret?
I believe everything happens for a reason, and as long as I am doing my best in whatever I am doing, I don't regret anything.

If you could change one thing in the chess world, what would it be?
Ban the Berlin Defence. ☺

What does it mean to be a chess player?
Travelling all the time! And you have to think before you act.

Is a knowledge of chess useful in everyday life?
I believe it is. Particularly in the case of non-professionals, it affects their lives in many positive ways.

What is the best thing that has ever been said about chess?
Chess is the Game of Kings!